PRACTICAL GUIDE TO Home Restoration

PRACTICAL GUIDE TO **Home Restoration**

by
William F. Rooney

VNR VAN NOSTRAND REINHOLD COMPANY
NEW YORK CINCINNATI TORONTO LONDON MELBOURNE

PRACTICAL GUIDE TO
HOME RESTORATION

A Van Nostrand Reinhold
Book / published in associ-
ation with Hudson
Publishing Company,
Library of Congress Catalog
Card Number 80-65300
ISBN 0-442-25400-8

Executive Editor, Robert J. Dunn
Book Editors, Sandra L. Beggs,
                Jane Williams
Art Director, Burt Sakai
Illustrations, Deborah Hopping
Graphics, Devouly/Lynch, Inc.
Producton Manager, Laurie Blackman
Composition, Wulf Schrader

Cover Photography: Val R. Hawes

Printed in the United States of America

Published by Van Nostrand Reinhold
Company. A division of Litton
Educational Publishing, Inc., 135 West
50th Street, New York, NY 10020,
U.S.A.

Van Nostrand Reinhold Limited
1410 Birchmount Road
Scarborough, Ontario M1P 2E7,
Canada

Van Nostrand Reinhold Australia
Pty. Ltd.
17 Queen Street
Mitcham, Victoria 3132, Australia

Van Nostrand Reinhold Company
Limited
Molly Millars Lane
Wokingham, Berkshire, England

16 15 14 13 12 11 10 9 8 7 6 5 4 3 2 1

CONTENTS

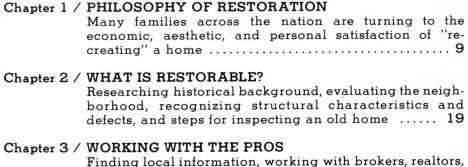

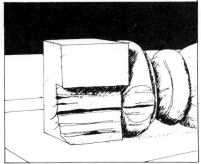

Preface

Nothing is more personal than the home in which we live. And few things age more gracefully than a well-designed house that, through the years, has received the hand of loving care.

Yet in our country today too many houses, streets, neighborhoods, and even cities are wasted by neglect. Some view this depressing condition as a national blight and reach for the time-honored wrecking-ball solution. Level the structure and rebuild in glass and chrome. Others, perhaps with keener eyes and longer memories, see these dated derelicts as a challenge for residential restoration.

Fortunately, we are beginning to realize that our architectural legacy amounts to much more than just log cabins and colonial saltbox homes. Our heritage developed on a regional basis from the original 13 Colonies and spread, mile by mile, to the South and West. Each family brought a personal concept of home as they carved out new territory, then modified this ideal to conform to varying climates, lifestyles, and native materials.

The result is a nationwide inventory of restorable homes ranging from a Midwest Prairie Victorian or the wrought iron and brick of New Orleans to the sun-baked adobe of New Mexico or the redwood and cedar-clad homes of the Pacific Northwest.

That's what residential restoration is about—reclaiming a dated dowager buried under years of neglect and restoring it piece by piece to its former dignity. Here you will find ideas, suggestions, and cautions to assist in solving both practical and decorative problems.

Giving new life to a dated dwelling can be an exciting adventure, full of surprise, frustration, and plain hard work. While you are restoring your home, you just may launch a chain reaction that sweeps down your street and throughout your neighborhood. Recapturing a piece of history can be a heady experience.

Chapter 1
Philosophy of Restoration

he formal definition of RESTORA-TION, often prefaced by "histori-cal" or "architectural," is the care-ful and meticulous return of a build-ing (usually on its original site) to its appear-ance at a particular period of time by removal of later work or the replacement of any missing earlier work.

Among the many meanings for the word PHILOSOPHY, you'll find references to a system of principles for guidance in practical affairs; wise composure in dealing with indi-vidual problems.

Now all of this may sound a little stuffy, but for our purposes restoration is best described as historical renovation—a recreat-ing of the original or earlier construction period with an eye toward present livability— all accomplished without destroying the ar-chitectural character of the home. Philos-ophy? Philosophy is simply the manner in which you, as an individual or family, ap-proach the restoration project.

Here, the accent is on discovering a badly used older home and bringing it back to its former dignity and charm. Sometimes it takes a cosmetic facelifting with a new coat of paint or newly applied siding. More complex pro-jects require a long-term commitment of time, energy, and enthusiasm. How deeply you be-come involved, how authentic your archi-

Photography: Norman Prince

At the left, a tall narrow Victorian style house in San Francisco blends a number of architectural elements into a well-proportioned statement. The bay windows and wide cornice with swag design contrast to the fish-scale shingle pattern. The use of horizontal siding on the lower two stories prevents the narrow structure from appearing top-heavy.

At the right, a careful and colorful paint application transforms a relatively ordinary Victorian into a small jewel. By accenting the period millwork, decorative shingles and turnings beside and over the porch, the owners were able to recapture much of the original charm. Wrought iron stair railings and grille on the porch window add safety and security to the simple, yet elegant restoration.

tectural reconstruction, and what compro-mises you make between historical accuracy and practical livability, all define your per-sonal philosophy of restoration.

As you become involved in restoration, you will run across a number of similar-sounding terms. While some of the terms are used interchangeably even among profes-sionals, each has a slightly different shade of meaning.

Reconstitution is involved when a struc-ture can only be salvaged by piece-by-piece reassembly at the original site or on a new site. This usually occurs when a building is damaged by disasters such as war, earth-quake, or flood, where most of the major components remain. Disassembly, reloca-tion, and reassembly are usually caused by a change in land use when buildings are re-moved for a new highway or dam.

Revitalization, as illustrated above, indicates the impact a single restoration, properly handled, can have on an entire neighborhood. Narrow Victorian townhouses, somewhat similar in design, are each supplied with an individual personality through careful attention to exterior details. One well-handled restoration usually encourages the upgrading of any street.

Recycling, as illustrated at the right, altered a small structure in Remsenburg, New York, into a charming weekend house. Originally it was a schoolhouse, Tuthill's Academy for boys, and later, the town post office. Exterior changes were minimal—a fresh coat of paint, attractive landscaping, new fencing, a welcoming post lantern and a gravel walkway.

Reconstruction takes place when a replica of a building that no longer exists is re-created on its original site based on archaeological, historical, and physical evidence. Old forts and early settlers' cabins are examples of reconstruction.

Recycling (sometimes called "conversion") is a relatively new term. The word implies adaptive reuse or a new function for an older structure. Barns, fire stations, schools and churches converted to homes are all recycled.

Rehabilitation, a term most often used interchangeably with renovation, involves modification or change to an existing building. Rehabilitation extends the useful life of the building through repairs or alterations while features of the building that contribute to its architectural, cultural, or historic character are preserved.

Remodeling means to model or fashion anew. The construction often includes major improvements, additions, and all structural changes and adjustments unrelated to any historical considerations.

Revitalization is a newer term, which usually encompasses several buildings, a street, or a neighborhood. Any improvements to a group of buildings or an area that generates new life and vitality to a previously run-down section qualifies as revitalization.

Preservation is the process of maintaining or treating an existing building to arrest or slow future deterioration, stabilize the structure, and provide structural safety without changing the appearance. This term is applied to those buildings that take on a museum-like quality and is not usually used to describe a family home.

Reasons for Restoration

For many individuals or families, buying a new home may make more sense than tackling a restoration project. Whether you buy or build, a new home offers complete freedom of choice. You can select the site or the neighborhood from dozens of options within your area. Then, working with an architect, builder, or plan service, you can create your dream house to fit the site or select from hundreds of floor plans, elevations, and styles of homes. The result is a new house, new appliances, a comfortable and workable floor plan plus the assurance that all construction, wiring, heating, and other utilities have been installed according to the latest safety and building codes.

On the other hand, a new home involves substantial expense—the cost of land, labor and materials, design and permit fees, and cost of money itself. Add to this, time for site

selection, design, construction, and approvals, the expense of maintaining a present home while your new home is under construction, and the time involved in making hundreds of decisions from the color of walls and carpets to the hardware styling for the kitchen cabinet pulls. Then there are the hidden but very real costs connected with new construction. Not all your present furnishings will be appropriate for a new home, which means you are likely looking at the expense of new drapes and furniture. A new lawn, shrubbery, and landscaping can run into substantial dollars. Rising taxes and unanticipated assessments for schools, sewers, and other utilities also contribute to additional costs.

A final consideration is travel time and cost. Most newer homes are located in the suburbs, which means additional driving to shopping, to work, or to take advantage of cultural and sporting events usually found congregated in downtown areas. If the advantages and disadvantages of new construction don't total up in your favor, then consider the idea of restoration.

Many individuals and families who have been through the restoration process chose this approach to housing because of several of the following advantages:

1. There is a surprisingly large inventory of restorable homes available at reasonable prices. Since the days of the early settlers, the wood-frame house has been the most popular form of construction. In almost every community across the country, there are frame homes in various styles, ages, and conditions. Any well-built house properly maintained does not wear out — at least for several hundred years.

In Madison, Wisconsin, the Forest Products Laboratory has conducted tests proving that when decay or other abnormal factors are not present, wood does not deteriorate in strength or stiffness from age alone for periods of 100 years or more. Further tests on timbers taken from Japanese temples 3 to 13 centuries old indicate that shock resistance is reduced after several centuries, but other structural properties are minimally affected.

Unfortunately, not all wood-frame homes have been protected against the deterioration of decay, insects, and weathering. Many have reached the point where restoration would be impractical. Nonetheless, there remain hundreds of thousands of homes, although outdated and lacking the modern conveniences, that are economically restorable.

2. To many people, a restorable home represents familiar surroundings in an established neighborhood. Tree-lined streets, landscaped yards, all utilities, roads, and

schools are in place. Predictable tax patterns, community shopping and social centers, and neighborhood closeness provide a feeling of comfort and confidence.

However, an established section of town does not necessarily imply a comfortable environment. Neighborhoods ebb and flow, some are deteriorating, others are barely being maintained. Crime rates vary. But the situation is a known factor and a little personal investigation will provide all the facts to make a buy/no-buy decision.

Another interesting phenomenon is taking place. Families are moving back into the neighborhoods in which they were raised. In many cases these young people have left home, completed their education, established their careers and families, then rediscovered their old neighborhood. A combination of practicality—more housing for fewer dollars, and nostalgia—a reaching back into an earlier and less complicated era, are apparently responsible for their return. And a house, one with character of its own, plays a big part in their thinking.

3. One of the most mentioned restoration benefits is space. Older homes usually represent more living area per dollar. Unlike the newer homes constructed on slab or crawl space, older homes often contain basements and attics which are finished or can be remodeled for extra bedrooms and family rooms. Existing floor plans offer formal dining areas and full-size kitchens; higher ceilings provide extra breathing room.

4. Although it takes a little planning, a restoration project can usually be conducted while the family lives in the home. If you schedule work on a room-by-room basis once the new wiring and plumbing have been brought up to code, repairs can be made over a period of time. This "live in while you work on" concept allows you to proceed as financing becomes available. By sealing off certain rooms, dust and odors can be controlled with minimum disruption to normal family living.

5. For the ecologically minded, restoration provides a certain psychological benefit. It is estimated that the average two-story older home contains between 15,000 and 20,000 board feet of lumber. Rather than demolish the original structure and replace it with new lumber and plywood materials, the restoration project can recycle the existing wood. Twenty-thousand board feet of lumber represents a substantial savings in new trees and the energy needed to convert them into useful building products.

6. The spector of long lines at the gas pumps and the increasing cost of fuel has placed a premium on automobile travel. Some

Photography: Leo Pinard

Older homes often provide extra living space when a basement or attic area can be remodeled. The small bedroom above was created from unused attic space. Steeply slanted ceiling under the roofline presents a decorating challenge, but with a little ingenuity, most families can easily solve the problem. Bright colors and a bold approach is the secret.

restorable homes are in rural and suburban areas but the vast majority are located either in or on the outskirts of large population centers. Here, public transportation or a short walk or drive in the family car puts you in close touch with jobs, retail stores, sports, and cultural events. With a restored urban home, you can be operating within a concentrated travel circle. Fewer miles generate a major savings in gas dollars and the time it takes to to commute.

7. Compared to buying a new home, can a restored home save you money? In all fairness, this has to be a "yes and no" answer, which must be carefully figured on the merits of each individual case. There are just too many variables for a pat answer. If, after a thorough inspection, your older home has

Photography: Norman Prince

When searching for a restorable house, it takes a keen eye and knowledge of architectural styling to separate a prize from the ordinary structure. The window detailing, shown above, was originally painted one unifying color. Fortunately the new buyers were experienced enough to see through the bland paint job and realize the detailing could be accented with color.

serious foundation problems, extensive rotted sections, badly outdated and inadequate wiring, heating, and plumbing sytems, if important parts are badly damaged or missing and if you lack the mechanical skills to do much of the repair work yourself and will have to rely on an army of professional craftsmen, then no, in the long run you probably won't save any money.

However, if your restorable home is in reasonably good shape, can be obtained for a reasonable price, can possibly qualify for National Register status, making special insurance, low-cost financing, and tax breaks available, and if you plan to handle much of the work yourself, then yes, you should be able to anticipate substantial savings compared to purchasing a new home. Each

situation must be weighed on the individual factors before any final dollar savings can ultimately be projected.

According to a recent article in *Business Week* magazine, "the cost of restoration can vary greatly, but generally it will run $50 to $100 a square foot, compared to about $30 to $40 for simple renovation or new construction." Gary Kray, partner in San Francisco Victoriana, a building restoration and material supply firm, estimates that restoring a Victorian facade in the San Francisco area will cost between 10 and 20 percent of the home's market value.

Your actual cost per square foot will depend upon the cost of the home, the extent of necessary repairs, your dedication to "historically accurate" restoration, and the amount of enthusiasm, free time, and skill as a craftsman you devote to the project.

8. The final restoration reason cited by many is not a practical or financial one but a collection of emotional and personal reasons. Individual tastes, nostalgia, a revolt against the assembly-line sameness of today's newer housing, a search for roots, and cultural heritage have been mentioned.

One Boston restorer summed it up by saying, "An old house develops the character of everyone who ever lived there. It has a different warmth, an atmosphere that a new house doesn't have." A Chicago restorer echoed the same sentiment with a slightly different twist. "To build the same house today would be impossible. It's not just the cost; there are no craftspeople who could build this." A New Orleans architect noted that, "People who want a restored home want it badly and are willing to pay." A West Coast restoration professional claims, "People are looking for their roots again and finding them in old houses. The demand just keeps right on growing."

To most people, restoring their own home represents much more than just creating shelter. It is a creative adventure, containing the excitement of a good mystery novel when time is taken to research the date and history of the home and its tenants. Restoration is like a giant scavenger hunt to track down missing millwork parts, that perfect doorknob for the dining room, or a local handcraftsman to reproduce authentic construction and decorative elements.

Restoration is not a part-time pursuit. Finding just the right home in an acceptable neighborhood, locating reasonable financing, analyzing the structural and decorative possibilities, and searching out competent architects, builders, and suppliers, all take an investment in time and energy.

Often, a good restoration job means almost letting the house determine its own future. Major changes or a drastic redesign are not always the best move. The small San Francisco Victorian house above required little more than minor exterior repairs, a new two-tone paint application to subtly reinforce the architectural detailing, and new brickwork with fresh landscaping.

The before and after photos above illustrate the impact of a well-chosen color scheme. The "before" house is a pleasant but ordinary structure that might be found on any average street. The "after" photo, however, gains its strength from separating elements, accenting details and changing the proportions—all done with color. Dark roof, neutral siding and light trim colors.

Who is Restoring?

The simple answer is, "Everybody is restoring." The restoration movement cuts across all strata of income, education, and background. Since restorable structures are found in all sections of the country, each area and almost every community now has at least a handful of successful restoration projects to inspire others.

The majority of restoration projects today are concentrated in the urban centers. These areas contain neglected jewels from a past era that beg to have life breathed back into their sturdy frames. Here also, potential restorers are faced with the toughest decisions reaching beyond the structure itself. The older sections of most big cities are usually the least attractive areas. Abandoned and dilapidated structures, poverty, filth, and high crime rates discourage involvement. Yet, surprisingly, it is here that restoration activity flourishes. Individuals and families are taking a second look at these neglected structures and responding to the challenge.

Sometimes local and federal governments have taken the initiative through rehabilitation or slum clearance programs. But more often, a homeowner who has completed his own successful restoration project has seen his neighbors respond to the lead by fixing up their homes, thus encouraging an entire neighborhood to turn itself around. At times the changes come quickly. More often, there is a long, hard struggle full of risks, disappointments, and frustrations. In the past, lending institutions have not looked favorably on investing in the troubled city core, building code officials have too often strictly enforced outdated regulations and the lack of competent restoration contractors and craftsmen have made the project difficult to complete satisfactorily within time and budget limitations. But things are changing.

Those first hearty few, those urban pioneers, have made their point. Older homes can be salvaged. Our architectural heritage can be preserved. Monies invested in restoring a home in poorer neighborhoods are dollars well spent—for the individual, financial backers, tradesmen, and suppliers.

Restoration Assistance

The federal government, upon investigating its urban renewal projects, discovered that much of the real rehabilitation progress was provided by the private sector, primarily individuals restoring their own homes. To assist interested restorers, the government has "popularized" much of its information originally designed for public and nonresidential rehabilitation programs. A relatively new 20-page booklet, **A Guide to Housing Rehabilitation Programs**, details a number of direct grants and loans available, describes various mortgage insurance programs, and provides information on eligibility requirements and application information. The final section lists the address of the state HUD area office for further assistance.

In addition, the government is publicizing information on its National Register of Historic Places program, explaining the criteria for listing and promoting the availability of historic preservation loans to support private restoration activity. The U.S. Government Printing Office in Washington is churning out a series of pamphlets and books covering all aspects of a restoration project. Some pieces, such as those from the Department of Housing and Urban Development and the Department of Interior, offer guidelines and checklists of do's and don'ts for your restoration; others like the 100-page

book **New Life for Old Dwellings** from the Department of Agriculture, Forest Service, which spells out in detail with photos and diagrams the steps necessary to properly evaluate structural problems, foundations, decay and insect damage, insulation, heating, and electrical situations, then how best to correct these problems in a workable manner. Quite a bit of solid information is offered at minimal cost.

Private historical and preservation groups have added to the available information. State and community groups, neighborhood organizations, and others now offer published materials covering everything from how to research your home's history to identifying the age of a structure through examination of the nails and hardware used during construction.

Following the national lead, local banks and even insurance companies are developing programs specifically designed to assist the restorer. These conservative organizations are now convinced that restoration is a more than worthwhile concept deserving of their participation.

Building professionals, starting with the

Appropriately enough, the traditional Salt Box colonial home, below, is located on a small hillside overlooking the rugged Maine coastline. The owners wanted a period home to showcase their extensive collection of fine antique furnishings and other "architectural" discoveries. This charming Salt Box was the perfect answer.

Photography: James Brett

15

architectural fraternity, have recognized the difference between new construction and restoration. A growing number of architectural firms are now specializing in rehabilitation, preservation, and restoration projects. Much of their work to date has been in the commercial and multihousing areas but more and more, the single-family restoration project is claiming its rightful place. Although commercial restorations usually represent larger dollars and perhaps more impressive results for the professional portfolio, architects are swept up in the enthusiasm and personality of home restoration.

Assisting the architect and structural engineer is a new breed of professionals—the building inspector who specializes in rehabilitation and restoration jobs. Through experience and interest, because of the growing need and expanding market, these experts are concentrating their talents on salvaging older structures. Developers, architects, contractors, financial lending institutions, and individual homeowners seek out the specialized knowledge of these inspectors, both before starting and during restoration.

There was a time when many contractors either refused to bid on restoration work or would only accept the job on a "cost plus" basis. In their experience, the average restoration project contained too many unknown factors and this made them understandably nervous. However, with the knowledge provided by experienced architects and building inspectors, more contractors today are willing and even eager to become involved in restoration work. Backed by a growing number of special subcontractors and suppliers, almost every community today has building professionals who can assist with residential restorations.

The growing interest of these individuals has created a professional talent pool of restoration experts who work with each other, trading information and contacts, in the restoration field. Articles and advertisements featuring these experts appear in publications such as **The Old House Journal, American Preservation**, and **Early American Life**. Your local newsstands or public library will probably have copies available. Two of the publications turn out annual "Source Book" or "Buyer's Guide" cataloging information on design and inspection services, sources for salvaged and new structural and architectural materials, and a listing of individual manufacturers producing tools, materials, and products of interest to the restorer. Information is available on topics ranging from heavy beams and wide floorboards to ornamental detailing, stamped tin ceilings, pull-

The increase in restoration activity has produced an interesting side benefit—the revival of handcraftsmanship. Above, a young craftsman at the Walton beveling and stained glass studio in Campbell, California, grinds glass on a horizontal wheel. When polished, the bevel reflects light rays in a jewel-like manner. Both clear and stained glass windows are making a comeback.

chain toilets, and custom paint and wallpaper suppliers.

One fascinating outgrowth of the restoration movement is the resurgence of handcraftsmen. Early restorers sometimes could not find a source for items needed for their own project so they produced them on their own. With a little research, a few hand tools, and trial and error at the basement workbench, a stained glass window was restored, a colonial lighting fixture produced, or Victorian gingerbread detailing made for a house facade. Friends admired the craftsmanship, a local newspaper article spread

Photography: Steve Marley

the word and all of a sudden the hobby blossomed into a full-time occupation. This coterie of young and not-so-young craftsmen provides an exciting part of the restoration scene. Most are dedicated and talented individuals who take pride and real interest in what they produce. They can be a gold mine of information for any restorer.

Is Restoration a Fad?

The answer is a resounding "No." The restoration movement is a well-established and growing part of the American housing scene. Two somewhat divergent examples may convince you that restoration is definitely here to stay.

At the professional level restoration is now being recognized as a legitimate career opportunity. A recent issue of **American Preservation** magazine listed among its pages several ads on the subject. Columbia University in New York was seeking a director for their program in Historic Preservation as part of their Graduate School of Architecture and Planning. Roger Williams College in Rhode Island ran an ad headlined "Make Preservation Your Profession," which detailed their on and off campus undergraduate program in historic preservation.

At one time an abandoned home was subject to destructive vandalism—windows were smashed, doors were shattered, plumbing and electrical fixtures were ripped from the walls. Now, entire stairways and paneled wainscotings are carefully disassembled, doors are removed or brass knobs, plates, and hinges stripped, stained glass windows are gently removed from the frames, and plumbing fixtures—including massive clawfooted cast-iron bathtubs—are salvaged. Restoration publications cite an increase in the number of "reward" ads seeking lost historical items. Law enforcement officials confirm the involvement of the professional criminal element when stolen items resurface thousands of miles from the original crime.

Restoration is obviously a permanent part of the American scene.

Chapter 2
What is Restorable?

inding the right home for your restoration project requires careful analysis, a fair amount of soul-searching, time-consuming detail work, and a large dose of perseverance. The "perfect" home does not exist, so the search is a series of structural, aesthetic, and financial compromises. But with proper planning on your part, the quest can be successful and well worth the effort. Establish criteria by which you can evaluate potential homes. Without such a checklist you will flounder in a sea of confusion. Your outline should include the following considerations:

1. Just what type of home do you need and want? Obviously, a single individual, a young couple, and a large family have different needs in housing. Each of them must decide what features best suit their lifestyle—the size of home, number of floors, kinds of appliances, and the type of floor plan.

2. The potential home's location is just as important. There are advantages and disadvantages to consider when comparing rural, suburban, and city living. The number and proximity of neighbors, schools, and churches, and distances to work, shopping, sports, and cultural activities are all factors.

3. The structural condition of each potential home must be analyzed. This can be done for you by a professional or you can tackle the job yourself if you have the experience to make an accurate appraisal. If you take an impartial, unemotional approach to house inspection, this can be the easiest part of the decision-making process.

4. Just how historically worthy of restoration is a house? Not every structure must be a

At the left, a modest house in Napa, California, shows great potential even while under restoration. The structure is basically sound and most of the decorative trim, although hidden beneath a single color of paint, is in good shape. With some minor repairs, burying of the electrical service lines and accenting of the decorative elements, this home can be a winner.

Photography: Ken Hilmer

landmark home where a famous personage was born, a battle fought, or an important treaty signed. Perhaps the house is simply a charming example of period architecture.

5. How much restorable house can you afford? The bottom line reality of your financial capabilities can quickly reduce your options. Be completely honest with yourself when weighing the merits of any older home. Add up the initial cost of acquiring the property, the expense of the restoration stage, figure in the cost of day-to-day operations, and include estimated maintenance costs.

6. The final consideration is a personal one. Do you honestly have the talent and temperament to engage in a long-term commitment to restoring a home? In some families, a week-long bathroom remodeling job creates

Restorable homes can be located in any section of the country. Below, in Boulder, Colorado, is a tiny 1,200-square-foot remnant of the mining town's heyday. The existing brick exterior was sandblasted and the wooden porch with curlicue support brackets was rebuilt. The porch roof supports a new deck off the master bedroom/bath loft, incorporated into the attic.

Photography: Karl Riek

Typical Home Sizes

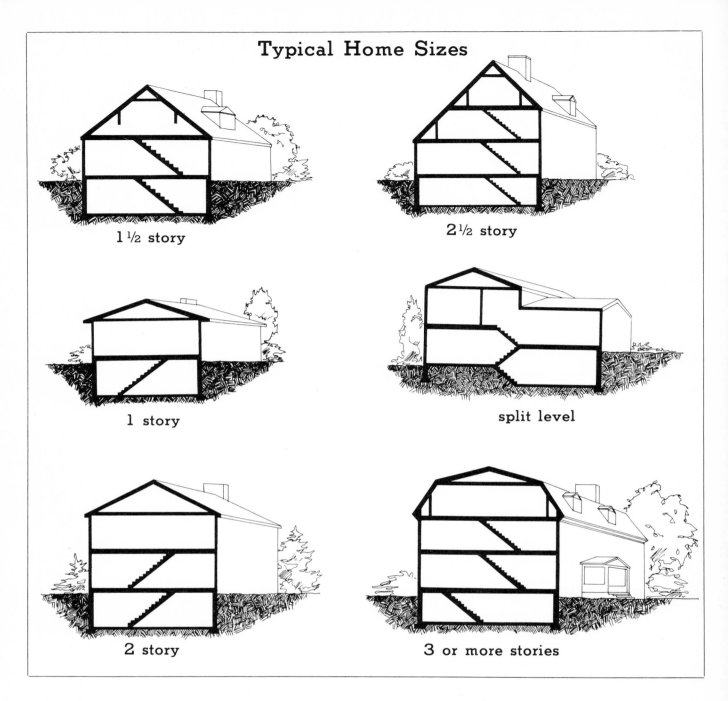

1 ½ story

2 ½ story

1 story

split level

2 story

3 or more stories

grounds for divorce. Are you and your family willing to tackle all the dirty, boring, and time-consuming aspects required in the typical restoration project? This question is one of the most important in making your final decision.

Style and Size of Home

There are certain minimum requirements that a home, any home, must meet to satisfy family needs. A single individual, a young working couple, or older retired folks can get by with less space than a growing family with four or five active children. How you use your home is just as important as the actual square footage. A lively, outgoing family with many friends and relatives in the immediate area needs an extra-large kitchen, generous en-

tertainment and outdoor living areas. A more sedate family may be content with minimal space if its personal interests and entertaining pattern call for more time spent away from home.

To help formulate your thinking when preparing your house-shopping checklist, it's a wise step to analyze various type homes and their advantages.

The single-story home has an obvious advantage for mothers with small children and elderly people—no stairs to climb. All the living is on one handy level. Since every room is at ground level, there is easy access to deck, patio, and outdoor living areas. Expandability is another plus in the single-story home. Provided the lot is large enough, extra rooms can be added on without disrupting the existing floor plan. Negative aspects? Without an excellent floor plan with good zoning, the one-story home can present a real privacy problem. Noisy children are omnipresent, evening entertainment disturbs sleeping children, and different age groups have difficulty separating individual activities.

The **one-and-one-half-story** house tends to be smaller and less expensive than some other styles. It is most often of a pleasing Cape Cod design with a sound floor plan. The extra space on the second level is viewed as an inexpensive "bonus," but too often, the upstairs rooms are tiny and provide little window area, and the steeply slanted ceiling reduces usable space. A major drawback is the proper heating and cooling of the second floor area. A heating plant with ample capacity is mandatory, and since the upper rooms are directly beneath the roof, extra insulation and proper ventilation are usually required.

Split-level or multi-level homes get mixed reviews. Originally designed to take advantage of hillside lots, the split-level lends itself to view property. Usually the entrance is at one ground level and a built-in garage may have access from the front or rear of the home. A patio often extends from the basement level, sometimes with a raised deck above. A well-planned home almost automatically segregates the working, sleeping, and living areas.

However, a poorly planned split-level can be a disaster. Jumbled room arrangements, a series of three- and four-step levels and no real sound control all lead to difficult living. Since the lowest level is the "basement" and the topmost the "attic," comfortable heating is nearly impossible unless expensive zoned heating controls are used. The room over the unheated garage, usually the master bedroom, can be cold without substantial insulation in the garage ceiling.

The **two-story** home is popular with good reason. It offers the most efficient living space on a minimum size lot and foundation. Bedrooms upstairs provide safety and privacy plus an ideal separation of sleeping areas from the living and working zones downstairs. Often combined with a basement, the two-story home has a lot of living space that is reasonably efficient to heat and cool.

Disadvantages may include limited access to the outdoors, and difficulty in adding extra rooms and stairs. Stairs can create energy-draining problems for young mothers and older persons. In addition, poorly positioned stairs too often create unnecessary halls and landings, which eat into usable living space.

Three- and four-story homes tend to accent the advantages and disadvantages found in a two-story structure—more space, more privacy but more stairs and additional heating problems. Multistory brownstone and townhouses do cram a lot of living on narrow city lots. They also offer one important extra consideration. Depending on the access and floor plan, these larger homes can offer the opportunity to create a separate apartment as rental property. Perhaps you hadn't considered becoming a landlord, but the additional financial help from outside income can be the factor needed to make your dream restoration a reality.

A Livable Floor Plan

Since each individual and every family establishes different living styles and operating patterns, it is virtually impossible to supply floor plan guidelines to fit each situation. However, there are a number of general principles that you can tailor to meet your specific needs.

From the exterior, an ideal floor plan should take the following elements into consideration:

The **front entrance** presents the first impression to visitors. It should be well-lighted, safe, and inviting. If there is a raised entrance, the steps should be in good repair and handrail firmly bolted in place. A covered porch to protect visitors from rain and snow is a plus. The front door should be a minimum of 36 inches wide to permit passage of oversized furniture, and should be solid with heavy hinges and hardware with either glass sidelights or a peephole to inspect visitors before unlatching.

The **rear or family door** is usually the high traffic entrance and should lead directly from the driveway or garage into the kitchen. This is probably the most important door in your home. Ideally, it is covered from the elements, well-lit, and secure. Here is the major highway for muddy children and dogs, the portal that feeds the groceries to the kitchen, and your prime access to the backyard.

Other entrances include garage and sliding patio doors (which should be security-proof), the door between an attached garage and the home, which is usually a solid core or fire-retardant door, and any basement doors. If you plan to take an active part in your restoration project, pay particular attention to the outside entrances. Will you set up your work area in the garage or basement, and what problems will you encounter in handling large sheets of plywood, gypsum panels, and long lengths of lumber and mouldings? If your only access to the work area is through a narrow back door or down winding stairs, consider the possibility of adding an outside basement entrance for these awkward, over-size items. It could be a good investment.

The **inside floor plan** demands special consideration. Picture in your mind how the house must operate on a day-to-day basis. A good floor plan is zoned to allow separate working, sleeping, and living areas. These three functions are both independent and overlapping, but a well-designed plan allows for any event.

Work areas include the laundry and utility areas, workshop, sewing room, and particularly the kitchen. All should be designed with adequate lighting and enough electrical outlets to provide for present and future power demands. The kitchen is the heart of most homes. It should be a pleasant place to work and eat in with sufficient storage space in base and wall cabinets, generous counter-tops, and a small eating area for informal breakfasts and snacks. The appliances should be arranged for best efficiency in the "work triangle formula" researched by Cornell University in their well-known study. The distance from the refrigerator to the sink to the range should form a triangle of between 12 and 20 feet. Conventional kitchen arrange-ments average between 16 and 17 feet around the triangle. The kitchen should be

Kitchen Work Triangles

Corridor

One-wall

L-shape

U-shape

U-shape/island

L-shape/island

handy to the rear door to receive groceries and adjacent to the dining room and living room for entertaining.

Living areas, family, dining, and living rooms, should be laid out so that family members can travel to different parts of the home without disturbing other activities. Children should be able to play, watch TV, or read while parents entertain. Where possible, the living areas should have easy access to an outdoor terrace or patio. The living room can be accessible to visitors with a handy coat closet by the front door, yet still isolated enough for a private conversation.

Sleeping areas, bedrooms and baths, are the private portions of the house. Adult bedrooms should be large enough to handle wardrobe storage, possibly a desk and chair as well as dressers and beds. Children's rooms can be smaller, but most provide space for study and play as well as sleeping.

Bathrooms should be arranged to accommodate two people at once, and even though small in size, must provide storage space for linen and toilet articles. Well-located baths are placed convenient to sleepers, yet handy to daytime activities. Large homes may have a bath for every two bedrooms and a half-bath near the back door—particularly handy for families with small children. Where space permits, tub-shower combinations make the most sense.

Storage areas are as important as any other feature in a home. If you are presently living in an apartment or newer home, you may be pleasantly surprised at the amount of storage space found in older homes. But don't be misled. Usable space, not just square footage, is the secret.

When detailing your storage needs, consider both live and dead storage requirements. Live storage, the space required for daily living, includes kitchen cabinets, utility and bedroom closets, medicine chests, shelves, and drawers. As a general rule, each person in the family needs a closet at least 24 inches deep and 48 inches wide. Well-designed closets usually feature ceiling-high doors, adjustable shelves, inside lights, and raised closet floors to keep out the dust. Older homes often have built-in storage areas, cabinets and drawers in hall walls, storage space under a built-in window seat, and occasionally drawers and shelving within a walk-in closet.

Dead storage space is for those seasonal or seldom used items—luggage and trunks, storm windows and screens, winter sports equipment, and garden tools. Basements and attics may not contain as much usable storage space as you first think. A damp basement is

Photography: Elyse Lewin

not the place to store clothing or furniture. Attics may handle a number of smaller items, but large and bulky objects are difficult to haul up several flights of stairs.

Before you start searching out potential homes, take the time to carefully think through the living patterns and needs of your family. Put your requirements down on paper and use this information as part of your house-hunting shopping list.

Selecting the Neighborhood

Through your own creative talents or with the assistance of an experienced architect, you can make major improvements in any home. But, being practical, there is not much you can do personally to make substantial changes in a neighborhood. Therefore, you pretty much have to live with existing conditions. Fully understand these conditions **before** you make your final housing decision. Surprises can be unpleasant.

Part of your research is common sense. Make a personal inspection trip. Drive through a potential neighborhood and observe the age, style, and condition of the homes, the condition of occupied and abandoned structures, and the general look and feel of the surroundings. Does the area seem to be zoned for single- or multi-residential use only, or is there evidence of commercial and light industrial structures?

As your investigation narrows down to several potential neighborhoods, travel the areas on foot for a closer look. Conduct your inspection trips during the week and on weekends to determine how the area functions, then consider an early morning and late evening trip to capture the full story.

A more formal investigation should include conversations with local realtors, bankers, law enforcement officials, and city planners. What is the present neighborhood

Through the efforts of the Carroll Avenue Restoration Foundation, the 1300 block area has become a monument to dedication and perseverance in Los Angeles. Several of the stately Victorian homes were completely restored, and others, from nearby locations, have been purchased, relocated and renovated. It all began when one young couple from New York fell in love with a neglected home.

condition and what are the trends? Are real estate values increasing, holding their own or decreasing? How serious is crime in the area? What is the present zoning classification and are down-zoning changes likely in the future? Are major highways being planned which will cut off or open up the neighborhood?

What is the level of school and church involvement in the neighborhood? Even if you have no school-age children or firm religious convictions, these factors are important. Local education and religion makes up much of the glue that binds a neighborhood society together.

Is there an active local neighborhood association or preservation group in the area? These are usually your best sources for honest, street-level information about what is really happening on a daily basis. No sugarcoating, just straight talk about the good, the bad, and the future possibilities. What does the school district spend per year per child, how are the classrooms staffed and teachers paid? What are local tax and assessment trends? Are bond issues being passed or defeated, and by what margins?

Compare the information gathered from the community professionals with that from the local neighborhood associations for a true picture of the total situation.

Do your homework. It's vital. And don't be easily discouraged. Many of the best restoration buys are in less than ideal neighborhoods and in what appears to be beyond salvage state of repair.

Inspecting Old Houses

Once you have narrowed down your choice of potential neighborhoods, you are ready to take the next, and probably the most important, step in your search for a restorable home — physical inspection of the most promising homes.

Before starting your inspections, there are several points to keep in mind:

A. Unless you are professionally qualified, it is recommended that you obtain the services of a competent house inspection firm. Check the Yellow Pages of the telephone directory under House Inspectors or Structural Engineers. At this stage, you *do not* want a House Appraiser, a professional who establishes a fair market value on a home based on the surrounding neighborhood and the structure itself. (You may want to have the home appraised later.)

B. Understand why you are making the inspection. Despite its present appearance, can the home be made livable for your family at a reasonable cost? How much time and money is involved? Familiarize yourself with local building code requirements so that you understand the improvements legally needed before the home is habitable. This can affect

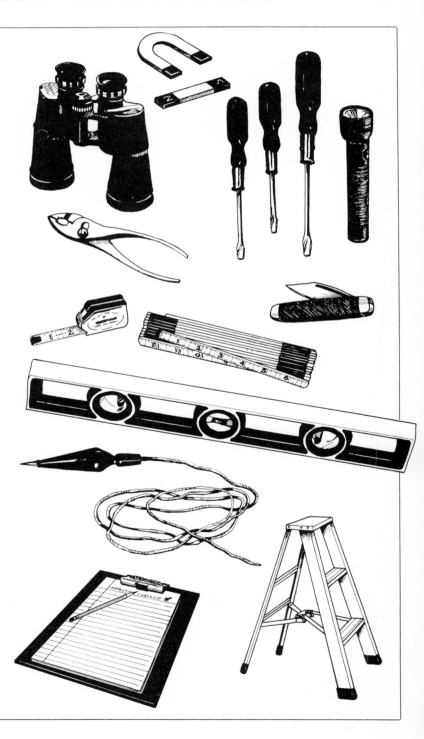

House Inspection Tool Kit

1. A pocketknife or ice pick used to probe for any rotted and decayed wood members.
2. A small magnet for a plumbing check. The magnet will stick to galvanized iron pipe but won't cling to copper, brass, or lead pipes.
3. A plumb bob and string (a 10-foot length of weighted line will do) to determine if walls, doors, and stairways are plumb and vertical.
4. A 3-foot carpenters level or a small marble or ball bearing. Are floors, stairs, and countertops level? Drop the marble and watch how far and in what direction it rolls.
5. A flashlight for poking into the dark, hidden corners of the basement and attic.
6. A pair of binoculars for a close look at the condition of roofing, flashing, gutters, and chimneys if you can't actually get onto the roof.
7. A 10-foot-long measuring tape (50-foot is even better) to record room dimensions and ceiling heights, as well as answer those nagging questions like, "Will our large sofa fit through the door?" and "Can the piano get down the stairs to the basement family room?"
8. Several size screwdrivers and a pair of pliers to pull switch plates, inspect the wiring, etc.
9. 4-foot ladder or step stool for above-eye-level inspections.
10. Pencil, pad, clipboard, and house inspection checklist to record information as you proceed.
11. Old clothes or coveralls and a pair of sturdy work gloves. Inspecting old homes isn't one of the cleaner projects; in fact it's downright grimy.

financial and construction timetables.

C. Be prepared to conduct a full inspection with all the necessary equipment. Your house inspection kit should include the items listed on the opposite page.

A Systematic Procedure

As you approach the house to be inspected, take a hard, impartial stance toward the job. What sits before you is not a charming Early American colonial or a classic San Franciscan Victorian. That structure is an old house. A second-hand home. A used dwelling. Look at it with the same skepticism you would use examining a second-hand automobile, an old washing machine, or a used table saw. What was the original quality, how has it been cared for over the years, what will it take to put it back into good working condition, and what will be the operating and maintenance costs in the future? If you can spot problems on the outside of the home, you can be almost certain that there will be additional problems on the inside.

Even with a checklist, you should take a systematic approach to your inspection. It is usually best to start with the exterior foundation, then outside walls and the roof. Later move inside and work your way from the attic down to the basement. Make notes, record information, and list additional questions as you proceed.

Foundations — The foundation supports the entire house and any serious problems here will have far-reaching consequences. Check the general condition of the foundation paying particular attention to uneven settling, large cracks, or deterioration that may allow moisture or water to seep into the basement. Examine brick and stone foundations for cracks and crumbling mortar. Poured concrete walls may have minor cracks which are not serious, but open cracks are another problem. Use your knife or ice pick to probe wood sills or beams resting on the masonry foundation. Wood rot and decay are caused by a combination of moisture and mild temperature. Damaged wood members will feel soft and spongy, are easily penetrated by a sharp object, and break squarely across the grain with little splintering.

Pull back all shrubs and vines growing along the foundation and check for any evidence of termites or carpenter ants. Earthen tubes on the surface of the foundation wall indicate where termites have built runways from the ground to the wood above. Carpenter ants do not actually eat wood but build their nests in it. Little piles of coarse sawdust along the foundation signal their presence.

Photography: Bill Rooney

While inspecting the exterior, particular attention should be payed to the condition of brickwork and mortar joints. The joints in the photo above have deteriorated to the point where a screwdriver can be inserted to the chimney flue inside. This condition is structurally unsound and presents a real fire hazard. A complete cleaning and repointing job will be required.

In some sections of the country houses are on pier-type wood post foundations. This construction calls for preservative treated wood members and should be carefully inspected for any signs of decay and insect damage. Porches are most vulnerable to decay and insect attack, since they are exposed to rain and snow, and are often in direct contact with the soil. Pay particular attention to the base of posts and columns where moisture collects and inevitably promotes deteriorating conditions.

Exterior walls — Sight along exterior walls or use your plumb line to detect any major bulges or out-of-plumb areas. Inspect doors and windows to see if they hang squarely in their frames and check the condition of the caulking around these units. Bulges and out-of-square components indicate foundation settling and may lead to expensive repairs.

What is the general condition of the exterior siding and trim? Are clapboards loose, cracked, or missing? Are shingles badly weathered or broken? Can missing decorative parts be duplicated from sections remaining intact on other areas of the home? Is the exterior paint surface in good condition? Excessive paint peeling, blistering, or curling usually indicates a water problem—either leaks from gutters above or lack of a vapor barrier within the walls.

Are joints between different materials— wood and masonry—protected with flashing and caulking? Brick work, particularly chimneys, demand special attention. Cracks in the masonry, loose or crumbling mortar, and

25

missing bricks require protective measures. The chimney should be supported on its own foundation and not by the framework of the house. Severely damaged chimneys represent a structural and fire hazard problem that can potentially lead to expensive repairs.

Roof — If you cannot get out onto the roof, use your binoculars to conduct a ground-level inspection. Note any sag in the ridge beam or rafter construction. Check the flashing in roof valleys and around the chimney. Water is the major enemy of any old house. Are the gutters and downspouts in good condition or are they clogged, rotted, rusted, or missing? Do downspouts have splash blocks to divert water away from the foundation?

Slate and tile roofing are excellent long-life materials, but broken or missing pieces are expensive to replace. Asphalt shingles are a more common roof covering with a life expectancy of 15 to 20 years. If the mineral granules on the surface appear thin and collect in the gutters, and the shingle edges look worn and ragged, you are overdue for a new roof.

Wood shingles and shakes, usually cedar, sometimes redwood, will normally last up to 30 years under favorable conditions. However, poor grades improperly applied, or moss or fungus growth in shady areas, cause reduced life. Broken, warped, upturned, and missing shingles are problem signs.

Flat or low-shaped areas with built-up felt roofing are especially difficult to maintain in sound, tight condition. Lack of good water drainage compounds normal problems. Any sign of cracking or separation in the felt roofing, blisters, bubbles, or soft spots indicates failure. If you are on a badly deteriorated roof, be extremely careful while in the process of conducting your inspection.

Interior spaces — During this portion of your investigation, you are not only concerned with the structural and mechanical aspects of the home but also with the general design and layout of the interior. Be realistic in your appraisal. In most any older home the kitchen is liable to be substandard, the electrical system underpowered, and the plumbing and heating resemble something out of the Dark Ages. Your job is to assess the conditions as you find them and then evaluate the cost and practicality of restoring them to acceptable levels. Based on your established criteria, can the home be made livable for your family within reasonable budget and energy restrictions?

Start in the attic, referring to your notes made during the roof inspection. Check for leaks around the chimney, valleys, and eaves. Dark water stains on the underside of the roof and along rafters indicate problems. Is the space adequately vented? Attic louvers or windows or screened vents in the soffits prevent the growth of mildew and fungus.

Most houses built before 1940 had little or no insulation. However, the recent interest in energy conservation may have encouraged the previous owner to upgrade the situation. Loose fill insulation between the attic floor joist should be a minimum of 3 inches deep in mild climates and 4 to 6 inches in colder areas. Check along the eave line to see if there is any indication that insulation was blown down into the wall cavity.

As you continue your inspection of the upper and main floors, observe the general condition of walls and ceilings. Water stains, peeling wallpaper, or rotted and loose plaster suggest serious leaks. Minor plaster cracks are inevitable in older homes, but crumbling and spongy areas will have to be removed and replaced. What is the condition of wallpaper and paint throughout the house? Multilayers of either wallcovering present a tedious stripping job.

Use your level or a marble to test the unevenness of floors and stairs. Bounce on the floor or stairs and check for excessive vibrations, window rattling, and gaps at the baseboard, between treads, risers, and stringers on the stairs. Pronounced vibration and bounce may be signs of expensive structural problems and repairs.

Glossary of Roofing Terms

Coverage — The degree of weather protection offered by a roofing material: single, double, or triple coverage.

Deck — The roof surface or platform to which roofing materials are applied.

Exposure — Specifically, exposure to weather: the distance from the butt edge of one shingle to another.

Flashing — Strips of metal or roofing material used in making watertight joints on a roof, especially in valleys or where inclined and vertical surfaces intersect.

Rake — The inclined edge of a pitched roof over an end wall.

Ridge — The apex of the angle formed by a roof, or the peak, where common rafters meet.

Valley — An internal angle or water runway formed by the intersection of two slopes in a roof.

Reprinted courtesy
Asphalt Roofing Manufacturers Association

Test the operation of all windows and doors. Do the sashes move up and down freely? Tight windows may be jambed out-of-square or painted shut. Too loose windows will require weatherstripping. Do the window frames indicate decay or water leakage? Check the plaster beneath such windows and the floor for water damage. All doors should swing easily without binding and have stout hinges and smoothly operating handles and locks.

Take note of the millwork and trim throughout the house. Window and door mouldings should be tight at the joints and firmly attached to the wall surface. Newell posts, banisters, and handrails should be in good condition and fixed in place. Missing sections may be difficult to replace or remake particularly if old patterns are no longer available. Fireplaces and mantels deserve special attention. Is the facing structurally sound and firmly against the wall? Does the fireplace appear to be recently used? Use your flashlight to determine if the damper is operational and if the chimney flue is clear, blocked, or badly encrusted with soot and pitch requiring the talents of a chimney sweep. A little-used fireplace or smoke stains on the front of the mantel usually mean a faulty fireplace.

Your notes should cover the general layout of the floor plan and its adaptability to your family's normal activities. Removing doors and repositioning walls can be done with care in an older home but the process requires careful planning and can be expensive. Determine how each room will function with your furnishings and family, then imagine how food preparation, small gatherings, and large family parties will fit into the plan.

Basement and mechanical areas — You can probably learn more about a house in a shorter time by a close scrutiny of these exposed areas. Do the basement and crawl space smell and feel damp? Check for indications of regular flooding, rust spots on equipment, mildew, or efflorescence on the walls. Has the space been used for storage, indicating it may be dry, or are items raised off the floor on wood or brick supports signaling possible moisture conditions? Are there floor drains or sump pumps in evidence?

Since basement areas are often unfinished, they can be an excellent yardstick to determine the type and quality of construction, as well as a spot where serious problems are most likely to occur. In the basement shown here, drainage problems became evident during a year of record rainfall. Walls and floors were sealed and a sump pump installed.

Photography: Leo Pinard

Here may be your first good opportunity to inspect the house's basic construction quality. Are beams and posts in good condition with tight, well-made joints? Use your knife to test the wood sill at the top of the foundation wall for rot and decay. Are the floor joists above straight and free of sag, or do homemade posts and columns prop up a weak floor system? Are basement doors and windows operable to provide access and adequate ventilation?

When you first enter the basement, turn on the heating system and allow it to warm up as you check other areas. Raise the stat setting above normal or outside temperatures and time the reaction. Electrical and hot air systems should respond almost immediately; steam or hot water radiators may take 20 to 40 minutes warm-up time. While the heater is on, visit each room and check the results. Are ducts clean or blocked? Do radiators hiss, steam, and leak? Do upper floors warm quickly and evenly or is the heating spotty throughout the house?

The heating plant itself bears close inspection. An old unit swathed in insulating wrap can be misleading. Some are so old that the wrap alone may be holding it together. Open the door and check the condition of the interior fire block and the general deterioration. Heating plants, 30 years old or more, may have been converted from original coal-burning furnaces and probably are in need of replacement. Use your stepladder to examine the state of heating duct work in the basement. Are the pipes and their brackets in good shape? Do duct baffles operate correctly or are they rusted open or closed? Is the hot air fan or blower system working properly? Around the furnace area you may spot a service card or sticker recording the maintenance dates of work performed on the heater. Take down the company name and phone number. Check with them later to determine if the furnace is covered by a maintenance contract, how much it costs, and their general impression of the efficiency and probable life of the furnace.

While in the basement, locate the water service entrance and shut-off valve. Then inspect other pipes, brackets, and valves to see if they are operating smoothly. Use your magnet to determine if the lines are galvanized iron or longer-lasting copper or brass. The magnet will cling to the iron but not copper, brass, or lead pipe. When scratched with a knife, lead pipe is soft and has a silvery color.

Now turn on several faucets throughout the house, and flush a toilet. Try the shower or bathtub. Observe any drop in water pressure.

	HYDRONIC (Forced Hot Water)	FORCED HOT AIR	ELECTRIC RESISTANCE
Heating Plant	Boiler	Furnace	Service Panel
Distribution System	¾" Tubing and Smaller	4" x 12" Ducts	Wire
Room Unit	Baseboard	Registers	Baseboard

Illustration Source: Better Heating—Cooling Council

Hydronic, or forced hot water heating is generated by a boiler, flows through pipes to baseboard room heaters. Forced hot air from the furnace is carried by ducts to individual rooms, while electrical resistance heating is controlled through baseboard units. There are pros and cons to each system depending upon energy rates in individual sections of the country.

Low pressure may be caused by lack of pressure at the main water supply and/or pipes badly clogged with scale. Plumbing fixtures that are badly stained, chipped, or broken may require replacement. Determine if your system is on a septic tank, cesspool, or city sewer and see how long it has been since it was last cleaned or inspected.

Your hot water supply is most likely from a cold water line run into a hot water or heating coil that is part of the furnace. A forty-gallon capacity is the minimum size needed by a family of four.

The final check covers the house's electrical system. When you add the power needed for electric ranges and clothes dryers to that needed for electric toothbrushes and garage door openers, most houses wired even 20 years ago are inadequate. Prior to 1940, most houses were equipped with 120-volt, 30-amp circuits. Later, into the early 1950s, a 60-amp circuit was common. The more adequate 240-volt, 100-amp service did not come into general use before the mid-1950s. Today, particularly in homes needing air conditioning, a larger 150- or 200-ampere circuit is definitely required.

Even if electricity makes you nervous and you don't consider yourself an expert in this field, you can still safely run a preliminary inspection on the system. You're looking for several key things: (1) How much power is being supplied to the house?, (2) How many individual fuses or circuits are in place?, and (3) Can additional circuits be added to the present panel or will an auxiliary board be necessary?

The main electric board is usually located near the electric meter. Turn the main or master switch on the side of the box to "off," then open up the panel. Inside, you will see a number of fuses or circuit breakers. Older systems may have as few as six or eight circuits, but a large house today may require between 15 and 20 circuits to be adequately and safely wired. Count and record the number of present circuits and note if additional unused capacity is left in the box. Just record the information for now. Later, if you are serious about purchasing this house, have the local electric utility company provide an adequate-wiring survey on the property. They will match up the existing service with your projected electrical needs and determine what additional power and circuits are needed. Most times, this survey is done free of charge.

While in the basement, note the general condition of the existing wiring. Do the wires appear old and frayed? Is armored cable or conduit badly rusted, insulation worn and deteriorated? Check the lighting fixtures and electrical outlets in the basement space. Do you have sufficient illumination and power to use a washer and dryer or install a workshop for the home handyman?

Now conduct a room-by-room survey of the rest of the house. Note the number, size, and location of outlets in each room. Ceiling lights should have a wall switch. Rooms without ceiling fixtures should have a wall switch wired to at least one outlet for a plug-in table lamp. Is there adequate lighting in hallways and stairwells for safe passage? Ideally, kitchen countertops should have outlets above for various small appliances, and bathrooms need outlets for electric shavers and hair dryers.

Don't be surprised if your electrical survey falls short of your present-day needs. Professional house inspectors report that, by today's standards, almost 85 percent of the older structures they investigate are inadequately wired.

By now, you will have a pretty complete picture of the house, its good points and troublesome areas. Before closing the door behind you and heading for a shower, run down your checklist again to be sure you have not overlooked any important areas. You can obtain a fairly complete checklist for surveying older homes that covers most of the above items from the Old House Journal, 199 Berkeley Place, Brooklyn, New York 11217. Ask for a copy of *Inspection Checklist for Vintage Houses*. The cost is nominal.

Researching Historical Background

Any home over 35 to 40 years old is worthy of restoration consideration. In today's chrome and plastic world, mere survival merits a certain amount of respect. Older homes, those that have withstood the daily abuse of several generations of active families, manage to project a certain solid character and inherent charm. Any structure is much more than just lumber, mortar, and pipes. The house's style, individual design and materials are part of the story; equally important is the human element. Who created the house, who owned it, and what events took place within its walls?

Researching the history of an old house should be undertaken early in the game for a number of practical and aesthetic reasons. The history helps establish an accurate value at the time of purchase and for later possible resale. A full understanding of the house is vital for restoration work in keeping with the style and tradition of the structure. Research can uncover important construction details to save both time and money in the reconstruction process. If you can document the facts, the house may qualify for inclusion in the National Register of Historical Places, making financial and tax breaks available.

Then there are those intangible reasons that add value to a home. After you have immersed yourself in the history of a home, the structure acquires a personality of its own. You begin to feel a kinship with previous owners and a sense of continuity is established. You and your efforts are not isolated events but become part of an enduring tradition. At times, during the tedious scraping of old paint or the dusty sanding of floors, this understanding of your place in history provides the incentive and encouragement to keep plugging away.

While conducting your research, keep in mind that you are seeking answers to basic questions such as:

1. How old is the house, when was it built, and what changes or additions have taken place over the years?

2. Who were the principals involved in its creation? The architect? Builder? Individual craftsmen? How was the house put together and what materials were used?

3. What is the architectural styling of the house and the history behind the development of the design?

4. Who were the original and succeeding owners of the house? What part did they play in the development of the community?

5. Most important, what did the house look like when first built and with later changes? Are construction plans, pictures, and old photos describing both the exterior and interior features available? And don't forget the secondary buildings, barns, sheds, and workshops, plus the landscaping and surrounding gardens that may be of historical interest. These are all part of the whole picture.

There are four sources of historical information to help with your research. No one area will give you all the facts you need, but by combining details from several sources you can often construct an accurate picture.

Documentary sources—Start your information chain at the city or county courthouse. Where money is at stake, records are kept. Check into real estate and tax records to determine the vital statistics on a house. Title records often quickly identify the original

owner and families who subsequently lived in the home. The tax assessor's office or building department may provide information on the architect, builder, original cost, zoning, materials, and specifications. With luck, the file may include a copy of the original plans, grades of material and possibly a photograph taken at the time it was first assessed.

This can be a time-consuming process, and various governmental agencies have different policies covering their records. However, city records can be a gold mine if you can gain access to them.

With a few basic facts, you can now expand your documentary search. Is the architect or builder still in business and what do their records hold? If any of the former owners were prominent in the community, try back issues of the city directories, files at the local public library, or newspaper "morgues" for business, civic, or obituary information. The local history department of nearby colleges and universities are additional places to continue your hunt.

While seeking details on a particular house, delve into the history of neighbors and surrounding property. Often, your parcel of land was originally part of another estate, which was later divided. Other homes in the area may be more fully documented than

Architectural Styling History

Research indicates that a home's styling can be as interesting as the structure itself. For instance, the mansard roof, popular in the East and Mid-West during 1850-1890, was named after the famed French architect Francois Mansart. Although the design had been used a century earlier, Mansart (1598-1666) employed it on several Paris hotels and chateaux. In contrast to conventional high-pitched roofs, the mansard roof has two slopes on every side with the lower slope approaching the vertical and the upper slope very nearly horizontal.

The mansard, usually pierced with dormer windows, provides a spacious and economical attic story. Part of its widespread use was based on its clean lines. Equally important to the frugal Frenchmen was its economy. At the time, taxes were levied on the amount of livable floor space in a home. The topmost area, immediately beneath the roof, was considered an "attic" and not subject to taxes.

yours, but this information can help you draw fairly accurate conclusions about construction, materials, and lifestyles of the period.

The older your documentary sources are, the more carefully they must be checked. You may be sure that you are talking about the same piece of property but double-check to make sure that the structure is identical. For instance, a fire may have destroyed the original house and you may be looking at a replacement built at a later date. Also, houses were often relocated in the old days. It may be that your house was originally built elsewhere and later moved to the present site. Check and recheck.

Another basic source of historical information may be the house itself. For houses built before 1840, physical evidence can be of value. Unless you are an expert, dating a house from physical evidence should be left to the professionals. They understand the problems of trying to draw a conclusion from any one piece of evidence or overlooking the various additions and improvements that are part of any older house's history. Remodeling activities may have either added or removed materials, and it was a common practice for early builders to "recycle" building parts from older homes. However, an expert can draw quite a bit of helpful information from an

existing structure. Hardware, nails, screws, door latches, hinges, have a well-documented progression from handmade to crude machines to the more sophisticated production equipment. Early nails were wrought and headed by hand, later nails were machine-cut but hand-headed, followed by machine-cut and headed nails, and the wire nails of today (common after approximately 1850).

Doors, windows, and millwork follow a similar pattern. Early material was shaped by various hand planes and later machine-made parts changed the design and construction of the elements. House framing and construction developed along defined time periods. Early houses were constructed of handsawn large timbers tied together with stout wooden pegs. After 1840, this system was replaced with the current balloon framing technique, using smaller 2x4 material nailed in place. Floors can best be dated by careful examination of the nails used rather than the width of the boards. The board width probably has more to do with economics than style. Wide knotty boards were obviously less expensive to produce than narrow, clear grade boards.

Interior finishing techniques and materials can sometimes help substantiate dating, but analyzing paint and plaster materials calls for specialized equipment and knowledge. The wood lath behind the plaster is often a better indicator of age. Here, again, there is a logical dated progression from hand riven or split on all four sides lath, to the "accordian lath" sawn on two sides, then split and partially separated, to the introduction in 1825 of the uniformly thick and wide rough-sawn lath we know today.

Sleuthing an old house for dating clues is fascinating detective work, but trained antiquarians are the first to admit that houses built after 1840 present a problem. Later construction does not present enough variation in methods and materials to be very exacting.

A third source for historical information relies on educated guesswork. Where no documentary evidence or little firm data can be found, you may have to fall back on inferred information. The style and layout of the home may provide some clues for dating the structure and defining the income, position, and lifestyle of the occupants.

American architectural styling has gone through accurately dated phases. In the East, colonial, saltbox, and Cape Cod designs were popular in the 1700-1830 periods. The Georgian period, with modifications, runs from 1760-1820. This was followed by the federal, Greek, and Gothic revival styles with Italianate, mansard, Queen Anne, and Carpenter Gothic periods coming later. As a rule,

American Architectural Styling

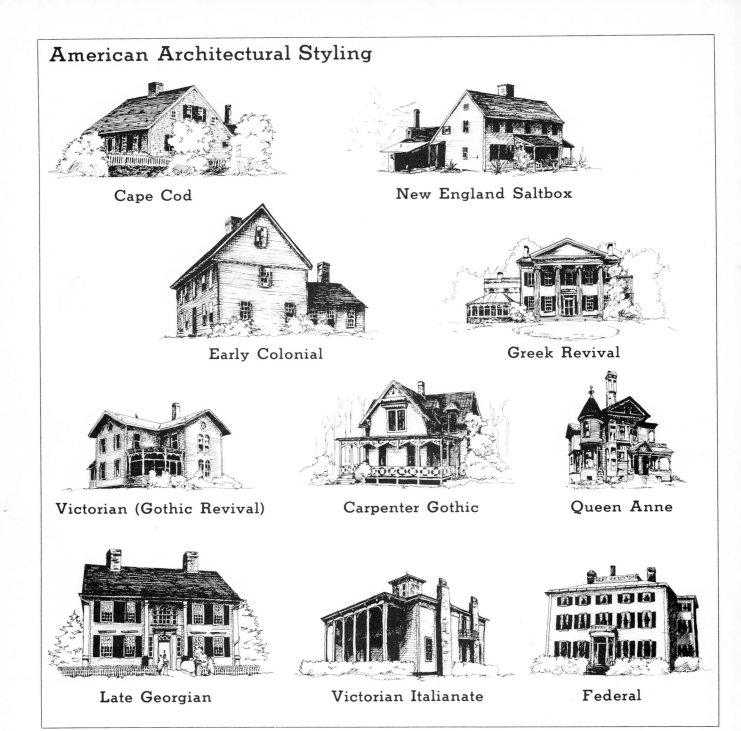

Cape Cod

New England Saltbox

Early Colonial

Greek Revival

Victorian (Gothic Revival)

Carpenter Gothic

Queen Anne

Late Georgian

Victorian Italianate

Federal

new styles first developed in the East and moved West and South. To complicate dating, styles usually originated in the major cities, then over a 20 to 30-year period spread to rural areas.

The final information source is one the antiquarians refer to as "oral history" — the spoken word gathered by interviewing people. Here, you reverse the procedure and start investigating the most recent occupant of the home. Who did they buy it from? Can the previous family be contacted by phone or letter? Neighbors or relatives of previous owners can be helpful.

With luck, family bibles and photo albums can be a gold mine of details. Ask permission to borrow and have duplicates made of old photos and records. Ask about how holidays were celebrated and how the home was decorated. What important events took place within the walls? What about the number and type of servants, farm and domestic animals, gardens, and landscaping?

Collecting oral history can do much to round out information on the human side of a house. Every time you run across a good source, conduct your interview and ask for additional leads. If you are not good at taking fast accurate notes, consider packing along a tape recorder to get down all those personal remembrances. Some of the dialogue will be folksy, some fascinating, and much may be irrelevant. Bear in mind that you'll have to make allowances for exaggeration and faulty memories. Cross-check all information with data from other sources and try to establish verification of the important facts.

Is the Home Restorable?

Both practical and personal considerations enter into the decision-making process. Start with your list of the criteria a home must meet to be acceptable for your family's needs and desires. Then, give careful consideration to the neighborhood. Can you be comfortable and feel relatively secure in this location?

Review all notes made during your house inspection. If there are no major structural problems, can the home be purchased for a reasonable price? Then, can the restoration be completed to your satisfaction within your budget limitations? The rule-of-thumb used by professionals indicates an older home restoration should normally cost no more than two-thirds of what a new home of comparable size should cost. Now add the cost of acquiring the older home and the estimated price for the restoration work. If this total is substantially higher than the value of surrounding homes, then your restored home may be over-improved and difficult to resell at a later time.

How much weight can you give to the information you uncovered during your historical research? Does this add any real value to the home or at least, has this pile of mortar, lumber, and pipes wormed its way into your heart? Sentimental value does not mean much to the finance company or a prospective buyer, but it should play at least a part in your final decision.

Now take a hard look at the entire financial picture. To the purchase price and restoration cost, add your operating costs for heat, power, and other utilities. Then, plug in an estimated monthly or yearly maintenance and improvement figure to arrive at your actual living expenses in the restored home. Can you handle the entire package from your monthly paycheck?

The final question may be the toughest to answer. Are you and your family ready to tackle a job of this magnitude? Can you live with the confusion, delays, frustrations, and minor victories that are part of any restoration job? Do you have the patience to wade through the dirty detail work, search out the right craftsmen and suppliers, and still maintain your sense of humor?

If most of the answers are positive, then you're ready to get serious.

Displaying Your Research

Once you have collected all the information on an older house, put the material to good use. Some families have typed up the results, combined the information with copies of records and deeds, old photos and newspaper clipping reproductions, and compiled a scrapbook. Others prefer to incorporate their findings into an interesting wall display where the material is on permanent view. To keep your display in the proper "historical feeling," ask your local photo studio to reproduce old prints in a sepia or brown tone rather than ordinary black and white. Avoid modern plastic and chrome frames. Instead scrounge around a few second-hand shops or garage sales to salvage inexpensive but ornate vintage picture frames. It's a simple job to mount the material, apply a few hand-cut mats or decorative borders, and produce an historical display for your walls.

Photography: Bill Rooney

Chapter 3
Working with the Pros

ne of the first and most important lessons learned by families involved in their own restoration projects is the need for outside assistance. Unlike a simple remodeling job, restoration demands a wide range of information, talents, and materials.

Locating the necessary experts, evaluating their competence to perform on your project, and learning to work smoothly with these professionals is part science and part art. Make up your mind early in the project— you will need outside help. There is no way one individual or family can possess the necessary background, current information, and mechanical talents to successfully complete the restoration by themselves.

Fortunately, experienced help is available and the list of knowledgeable experts grows daily. It is even easier to locate these individuals today than ever before. Many now advertise their talents and materials in the growing number of magazines and periodicals devoted to restoration. Various groups are sponsoring local seminars and conventions to bring the professionals into contact with the general public. In Chicago, Mayor Jane M. Byrne is lending the support of her office to promote City House, a Home Improvement Fair for Older Houses, presented by the Commission on Chicago Historical and Architectural Landmarks. The aim of the fair is to help citizens learn how they can create attractive, stable neighborhoods and discover the products and techniques that are appropriate for their home restoration projects.

In Boston, a different approach was taken. Television producer Russ Morash, who also produced Julia Child's cooking and Crockett's Victory Garden programs, conceived the idea for a "how to" house restoration program while working on his own 1851 farmhouse near Boston. The star of "This Old House," a 13-week program on WGBH, was a dilapidated 1860s' house in Dorchester's Meeting House Hill section. The house was purchased by the station and the program sponsored by several local financial institutions and Grossman's, a major building material supplier headquartered in Braintree, Massachusetts.

The rambling three-story structure served as the set for the various home repair

Left, television producer Russ Morash of WGBH, Boston, surveys the condition of an 1860s' house in Dorchester, Massachusetts, selected to star in the 13-week "This Old House" program. Inadequate lighting and wiring, damaged walls, scarred millwork, and jumbled floor plan all contributed to the restoration problems/opportunities explored in the series.

The upstairs bathroom of the TV house, shown to the right, illustrated typical restoration problems. An earlier remodeling had degenerated into water damaged walls, missing tile, broken and antiquated fixtures, plus minimal heating and lighting. The challenge was to correct these structural and aesthetic faults during the 13-week series.

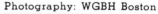
Photography: WGBH Boston

and restoration projects. Bob Vila, president of a local restoration firm, was the program host. In the early segments, Vila toured the house and property describing the work to be done while interviewing a house inspector, heating specialist, and a realtor to gain insight into the problems and opportunities available in the old structure. In later programs, scaffolding was erected and exterior repairs on the roof, gutters, and clapboard siding demonstrated. Inside, Vila explained what happened during demolition, and how and why walls were torn down.

Featured during subsequent weeks were step-by-step instructions on painting, caulking, stripping, sanding, electrical wiring, and landscaping as well as interviews and discussions with various restoration specialists.

The reception to "This Old House" has been so favorable that plans for turning the program material into a book and syndicating the 13-week series are being seriously discussed.

But if you don't live in Chicago or Boston, help is still available in your community.

Finding Local Information

Since your first step may be locating an acceptable neighborhood and a specific house for your restoration project, a visit to several local neighborhood associations can save you a lot of time and leg work. These organizations are your best source for current street-level information on what is happening in various parts of your community. The staffs are extremely knowledgeable about conditions in their immediate neighborhood, and since they have nothing to sell, can be helpful in supplying information.

Most neighborhood associations have current area maps and can quickly point out schools, churches, and shopping locations. They also are familiar with zoning in the immediate area, traffic patterns, planned changes in highway and bridge construction, neighborhood crime rate trends, tax assessments in the area, and a number of other important bits of information that are not available elsewhere.

Since the staff usually lives in the area, they have a first-hand understanding of the emotional makeup of the neighborhood. Are the residents maintaining and improving their property or are the homes falling into neglect? Are school bond levies being passed or defeated? How is the area changing, and is it for the better or worse?

In addition to statistical information, the local association staff can be a gold mine of practical data. They may know of several houses on the market or about to go on sale.

Photography: From the archives of San Francisco Victoriana

Locating the right structure for a restoration project is part luck and part hard work. Above, an extremely narrow Victorian house in San Francisco, being shown to a prospective buyer, combined an acceptable neighborhood with a sound structure at a reasonable price.

They are familiar with the realtors who tend to specialize in a particular neighborhood. They usually know the local bankers and financial organizations and their present feelings about investing in the area. They can probably recommend housing inspectors, builders, salvage yards, supply houses, and individual craftsmen, from specialists in stained glass to architectural millwork, who have done business with local residents.

Take a loose-leaf notebook along, ask questions, and jot down answers and information. Do they have any historical information on the area or can they give you a name at the historical society? Who should you deal with at City Hall for zoning and building code problems? Which architects understand restoration projects? Who insures most of the homes in the neighborhood?

Local associations are the experts in their immediate section of town and have a good idea about activities outside their local boundaries. In Portland, Oregon, for instance, there is a collection of six neighborhood associations that have banded together to handle zoning and street problems on the west side of town. Each office can put you in touch with their counterpart in another section of the city.

While the neighborhood association may know of several houses for sale in the area, chances are excellent that the houses will neither fit your specifications nor your pocketbook. Most restorers are not that lucky. You would be better off, once you have decided upon an area, to get the names of several brokers or realtors who are active in the area from the association staff.

Brokers and Realtors

You can find a restorable house without the assistance of a professional, but it takes time and work on your part. You can scan the newspapers, hoping the real estate section will produce a lead on the right piece of property, or talk with your friends and neighbors who may know of a house on the market. Then there are the phone calls for appointments, hours of driving around, and the possible frustration of trying to locate and deal with absentee landlords. A broker or realtor can save you days and miles. In fact, you should consider using several professionals to speed your search.

Although the terms "broker" and "realtor" are sometimes used interchangeably, there is a difference you should be aware of. A real estate broker is an individual licensed by the state as qualified to deal in real estate transactions. A broker may be called a salesman or agent, but he usually owns the firm, and may have licensed salesmen working for him. There are over 500,000 licensed brokers in the country, which averages out at one for every 10 or 12 houses. If this figure seems high, remember that many brokers may be housewives, retired, weekend or part-time salesmen.

Realtors are licensed brokers but also members of the National Association of Real Estate Boards and members of one of the more than 1,400 local real estate boards in the country. Approximately 15 percent of all brokers are legally qualified to call themselves realtors.

The fact that an individual carries the title of realtor does not mean he is any more competent, efficient, or honest than a broker. Many brokers have years of experience, large organizations behind them, and fine reputations. However, if you are dealing with unknown individuals, it is generally safe to assume a realtor is a full-time professional who earns his livelihood from daily real estate transactions.

The only effective way to deal with a real estate professional is with complete honesty. Fully explain the neighborhood, style, size, number of rooms, and any special features of the house you are looking for. Let him know those things that are not acceptable, and give him a reasonable idea of the price you are prepared to pay. The more specific you can be, the better service he can provide.

Some people are reluctant to engage a professional because they resent the idea of paying the 5 or 6 percent commission. Although the commission may be included in the final price, it is actually the seller, not the buyer, who pays the real estate commission. Furthermore, if the broker, through his understanding of neighborhood values and tax assessment trends, knowledge of various houses available, and complete comprehension of your needs and desires, locates the "perfect" house quickly, then don't begrudge him his commission. It is a paradox, but the top brokers seem to spend the least time closing a transaction. You are buying his years of experience, not hiring him by the hour. Just keep in mind the number of false leads you didn't have to follow up, and the houses you didn't have to inspect and then later reject.

Brokers, like the rest of us, are human. Realize that they are experts in a relatively narrow field. Most will supply honest answers to standard real estate questions, but it is wise to double-check this information with another source. Occasionally, they get carried away with their own enthusiasm and start making comments outside their field. When you hear statements like "those new shingles . . . ," when to your eye it appears to be an ordinary nine-year-old roof, or "this sturdy construction," or sweeping comments about how easy it will be to "knock out those walls and expand the kitchen," then remember, you are listening to a real estate broker and not a construction professional.

There is no reason why you should let yourself be pressured into making a hasty decision. Buying and restoring an older house is a major investment in dollars and time, so you should investigate thoroughly before making up your mind. And before you sign anything, be sure to have the documents reviewed and explained to you by a competent real estate lawyer. Not only can your broker assist you in finding and negotiating for a house, but most can also recommend several contacts to help you find the best financing, insurance agent and knowledgeable lawyer. Ask for these names and record them in your notebook along with all the other information you've collected.

SOURCES TO HELP YOU GET STARTED:

- Your Local Board of Realtors for information on Realtors Neighborhood Revitalization Program, and firms specializing in historic properties
- Financial institutions
- Homeowners associations
- Local historical societies or preservation groups
- City departments such as planning, housing, community development, or the treasurer's or mayor's office
- State Historic Preservation Officer
- U.S. Department of Housing and Urban Development, Washington, DC 20410
- Office of Archaeology and Historic Preservation, National Park Service, U.S. Department of the Interior, Washington, DC 20420
- Neighborhood Housing Services, Urban Reinvestment Task Force, 1120 19th Street, N.W., Suite 600, Washington, DC 20036
- National Trust for Historic Preservation, 740 Jackson Place, N.W., Washington, DC 20006

Historical Research

The best time to conduct your historical research is after you have located a potential house, but before you have actually purchased the property. This will give you the opportunity to investigate the true worth of the house before you have signed the papers. Establishing the historic value of a structure will be a big help in formulating your plans, obtaining the best financing package, and completing an authentic restoration project.

In Chapter 2 we discussed sources for obtaining historical information—neighborhood associations, the tax department or building office at City Hall, history departments of local colleges, files at newspapers or historical societies, long-time neighborhood residents, etc. How you deal with these professionals will have a big bearing on how much information you uncover, and how quickly and easily the search is conducted.

Keepers of historical information are not known to be overpaid; some may be working on a volunteer basis, and others operate from a civil-servant mentality. But there are some simple methods that will make the research task easier and more pleasant for all concerned. Your initial approach is the key to your success.

Start off by treating them like people. Rather than storming into the office demanding information, take a few minutes early in the conversation to explain what you are after and why the information is important. Let your enthusiasm show through, and get them involved in your problem. Bring along copies of whatever data you have already collected and a list of questions to guide them in their search.

Record phone numbers and names of everyone you talk with, and relay any new-found information back to these individuals to assist them in your search. Put things on a one-to-one basis. Talk with people, not offices or titles.

In some cases, you are better off not dealing with the top people. Department heads and managers may be better administrators than historians. Ask if someone on the staff lives in the area you are investigating. If you find someone, you may discover that your status has changed suddenly from a "customer" to a potential "neighbor." That relationship can pay big dividends.

Seek out the long-term employees. In most cases these are the individuals who really know where the dusty maps, aging photos, and hidden records are buried. With a friendly approach and an understanding of your needs, these people can rise to the challenge and devote many productive hours answering your historical questions.

Thorough historical research is time-consuming. If you are afraid the house may be sold to another buyer, or if you have a limited earnest money agreement or option, you may be wise to consider obtaining the services of a professional organization to conduct your research. Now you have professionals dealing with professionals, and a quicker, more thorough job is possible. A number of organizations are available in major cities and, one of the best known, the Consulting Services Group of the Society for the Preservation of New England Antiquities, is headquartered in Boston.

Much of the work done by the Consulting Services Group is for cities and historical societies, but they include private homeowners among other clients. The Group, founded in 1973, is composed of architects, draftsmen, scientists, architectural conservators, and historians. The variety of services includes documentary research on historic buildings, surveys of early buildings with reports on their structural conditions, and architectural history, and identification of specific features worthy of preservation. In addition, they can provide advice on planning, landscaping and streetscaping preservation. Their technical services cover analysis of historic mortars and advice on cleaning, repair and repointing of early masonry structures, microscopic and chemical analysis of early paints to match and reproduce historic paint colors, plus nondestructive X-ray examination of structural parts without removing surface elements. Finally, the Group offers consultation services on wallpaper, carpeting, and furnishings.

Registering Historical Properties

In the course of your research, you may uncover information that leads you to believe that your house may qualify for a listing in The National Register of Historic Places. The law that created the official list in 1966 stated that eligible properties include places of state and local, as well as national, importance.

A recent article in *American Preservation* magazine began with the question, "What do a Rhode Island carousel, an Alaskan totem pole, the home of abolitionist-writer Frederick Douglas, and New York's Brooklyn Bridge have in common?" The answer, obviously, was that they all have been deemed worthy of preservation and are listed in the National Register of Historic Places. Today, the list includes approximately 15,000 properties. The majority are individual listings, but some cover historic districts and neighborhoods.

Both the home and small smokehouse shown below are 18th-century buildings that were owned by the Reverend John Bracken, rector of Burton Parish Church for 45 years, and at one time the mayor of Williamsburg, Virginia. Period landscaping enhances the space in the service yard area in the rear of the house.

Photography: Colonial Williamsburg

Form No. 10-300 REV. (9/77)

UNITED STATES DEPARTMENT OF THE INTERIOR
NATIONAL PARK SERVICE

NATIONAL REGISTER OF HISTORIC PLACES
INVENTORY -- NOMINATION FORM

FOR NPS USE ONLY

RECEIVED

DATE ENTERED

SEE INSTRUCTIONS IN *HOW TO COMPLETE NATIONAL REGISTER FORMS*
TYPE ALL ENTRIES -- COMPLETE APPLICABLE SECTIONS

1 NAME

HISTORIC

AND/OR COMMON

2 LOCATION

STREET & NUMBER
_NOT FOR PUBLICATION
CITY, TOWN
CONGRESSIONAL DISTRICT
_VICINITY OF
STATE   CODE   COUNTY   CODE

3 CLASSIFICATION

CATEGORY	OWNERSHIP	STATUS	PRESENT USE
_DISTRICT	_PUBLIC	_OCCUPIED	_AGRICULTURE _MUSEUM
_BUILDING(S)	_PRIVATE	_UNOCCUPIED	_COMMERCIAL _PARK
_STRUCTURE	_BOTH	_WORK IN PROGRESS	_EDUCATIONAL _PRIVATE RESIDENCE
_SITE	**PUBLIC ACQUISITION**	**ACCESSIBLE**	_ENTERTAINMENT _RELIGIOUS
_OBJECT	_IN PROCESS	_YES: RESTRICTED	_GOVERNMENT _SCIENTIFIC
	_BEING CONSIDERED	_YES: UNRESTRICTED	_INDUSTRIAL _TRANSPORTATION
		_NO	_MILITARY _OTHER

4 OWNER OF PROPERTY

NAME

STREET & NUMBER

CITY, TOWN   STATE
_VICINITY OF

5 LOCATION OF LEGAL DESCRIPTION

COURTHOUSE,
REGISTRY OF DEEDS, ETC.

STREET & NUMBER

CITY, TOWN   STATE

6 REPRESENTATION IN EXISTING SURVEYS

TITLE

DATE
_FEDERAL _STATE _COUNTY _LOCAL
DEPOSITORY FOR
SURVEY RECORDS

CITY, TOWN   STATE

Can just any old structure qualify? Not necessarily. The National Register criteria for evaluation are stated as:

The quality of significance in American history, architecture, archaeology and culture is present in districts, sites, buildings, structures, and objects that possess integrity of location, design, setting, materials, workmanship, feeling, and association, and:

A. that are associated with events that have made a significant contribution to the broad pattern and spectrum of history; or

B. that are associated with the lives of persons significant in our past; or

C. that embody the distinctive characteristics of a type, period or method of construction or that represent the work of a master, or that possess high artistic values or that represent a significant and distinguished entity whose components may lack individual distinction; or

D. that have yielded, or may be likely to yield, information important in prehistory or history.

Unless a treaty was signed in your living room (A) or unless your house sits atop an old fort or Indian burial ground (D), your best hope for inclusion in the Register falls in categories B or C. Properties associated with historically significant people generally include well-known national or local politicians, artists, inventors, or business leaders. Sometimes, a strange twist may qualify a structure, like the Jacob Kamm House in Portland, Oregon, which was built for a local steamboat engineer. Thanks to the installation of a ship's boiler, the house has the distinction of being the first centrally heated structure in the territory.

Residential properties of architectural significance range from river plantation homes to city mansions. But many are surprisingly modest structures. As long as they represent a specific building type or date from a certain stylistic period, they may qualify. The bungalow or saltbox house, federal, Queen Anne or Art Moderne styles, or construction examples such as adobe, half-timber, or poured-in-place concrete may qualify to be listed.

There can be substantial benefits from having your property listed in the National Register. You receive formal recognition of the historical qualities of the property, which enhances the resale value, and you are eligible for matching grants-in-aid funds from the Department of Interior. It also offers a measure of protection from intrusion by federally funded renewal projects. In addition, the Tax Reform Act of 1976 and the Revenue Act of 1978 provide additional financial benefits. There is often eligibility for 50 percent matching financial grants for restoration work and loan guarantees, which encourage lending institutions to finance your restoration activities.

If research indicates your property may qualify for listing, contact your local preservation groups or historical societies or the State Historic Preservation Officer for information and a copy of the eligibility forms. The paperwork may well be worth the extra time you invested.

House Appraisers and Inspectors

House appraisers judge the market value of a house and inspectors judge the physical condition of the structure. Both may be important professionals to consider before you actually purchase the restoration property.

The house appraiser can assure you that the seller is asking a reasonable price for a particular house in a particular neighborhood. He is an expert in current real estate trends and property evaluation. Let him know of your restoration plans and he can guide you in understanding the dangers of "overimproving" your property. Although the asking price may be realistic, if you plan major repairs and improvements, your total dollar investment may raise the evaluation far above your surrounding neighbors. For instance, a $50,000 house that takes an additional $30,000 or $35,000 to restore will prove difficult to resell when the surrounding homes are valued at $50,000 to $60,000.

A house appraiser may be part of a real estate firm, on the staff of a bank, lending institution, FHA or VA office, or an independent appraiser. Check the Yellow Pages of the phone book under Appraiser or Real Estate Appraiser to find a qualified individual. It pays to check his reputation with customers or some of your other contacts.

The appraiser can help you determine the value of the house, but he is not, in most cases, a structural expert. For this advice, you should seek out a qualified house inspector. He may be an architect, former builder, or engineer. Be sure he is familiar with the mechanical aspects—plumbing, wiring, heating systems—as well as the structural details. Look under Building or Home Inspection Services in the Yellow Pages.

For the wealth of information he can supply, the professional inspector's fees are reasonable. Depending on the size, condition, and location of the house, charges run from $75 to $150. The process may take several hours for an experienced inspector with a detailed checklist. Inspection reports are usually returned within three days to one week.

Again, let this professional in on your planning. He should be aware of your intentions to make any major changes, rewire or replumb, tear out walls, or add a porch. If the inspection uncovers problems, he usually provides a rough estimate of repair costs to restore function and livability to the structure. His biggest advantage is the fact that he is an independent expert, not trying to sell you anything, but providing a dispassionate and factual report on conditions as he finds them. His inspection report can give you a rough idea of the size of the total restoration project and, perhaps, supply a little bargaining leverage when negotiating with the seller of the house.

Up to this point, things have progressed in a fairly logical sequence. You have met and worked with a number of professionals and are beginning to have a feel for the problems and possibilities involved in your restoration project. You have selected a neighborhood in which you can be comfortable,

discovered a likely house, researched its historical background, and conducted a general house inspection.

Now, however, the pace picks up at an alarming rate. Your cast of professionals grows, details and decisions pile up, and the comfortable step-by-step process breaks down into simultaneous and overlapping activities. It is a crucial and complex time, but you can work your way through the maze of facts, figures, and options, estimates and conflicting opinions. Other people are doing it successfully every day.

Your task now is to estimate the total cost for the project, obtain your financing, retain

"A trickle of water entered at the roof," comments a certified building inspector, "then all the wood beams dry rotted. A minor problem that could have been easily fixed now will cost over $1,000 in total wall repairs." A good house inspector can give you a rough idea of the size and cost of a total restoration project.

Photography: Lee Foster

a lawyer to assist you with contracts, purchase the property, and retain an architect or engineer to plan the restoration and work out all the details. Then you must decide if you will attempt to act as your own general contractor or if you will hire a builder, contractor, or remodeler to do the actual restoration work. Several bids should be obtained and a decision made on the final contractor or subcontractors involved in the project. Then you will undoubtedly take part in specifying and ordering various construction and decorative materials, as well as seeking out those individual local craftsmen who will apply their custom work and personal touch to your home.

Estimating Costs

Ideally, before you obtain your financing, before you actually purchase the property, and before you are fully committed to the restoration project, you should determine the total cost as accurately as possible. It is vital that you understand the scope of your involvement. Your total costs must include the expense of buying and restoring the house, plus operating and maintaining the house once it is completed. Some are one-time costs, others have a limited time span, and some are perpetual (or at least they seem that way). Some expenses, such as your mortgage interest, are at a fixed rate, while others, like operating and maintenance costs, are subject to inflation. Estimating the cost of owning a home isn't all that complicated, but it does require time and attention to detail.

The cost of purchasing the house should include the price of the property, the professional inspection fee, legal fees for the attorney, financing costs for broker's fee, points of interest, and closing expenses for title search, mortgage insurance, etc.

Estimated restoration costs should include the architect's fee, labor and material, construction insurance, permits, and utility costs for water, electricity, and heat needed during construction. If you are not living in the house during restoration, then you must add the "carrying costs" into your total. On a restoration project, it is not unusual for a year or more to pass before the house is occupied. It may take six months for the inspection, planning, and obtaining the financing, with another six months or more for construction time. Mortgage and real estate taxes must be paid; insurance and utility expenses, as well as the cost of maintaining your present home, must be calculated.

Operating and maintenance costs are the most difficult to pin down accurately. As Marsh Trimble, publisher of *Professional Builder* magazine, stated in his industry newsletter, "The cost of operating a home in the last ten years (1970-79) has increased nearly 150 percent. The number one culprit in advancing costs were maintenance and repairs—up 180 percent on new homes, 191 percent on existing homes. Next in order of higher costs were insurance, up 174 percent, real estate tax, up 157 percent, and utilities, up 123 percent."

Your estimated operating and maintenance costs include mortgage payments, insurance, taxes, water, sewer, and trash collection fees, electric, gas, and oil utilities, as well as anticipated minor and major repair expenses (new roof, repainting every five years, etc.).

Once you have a grand total figure, break this down as best you can into equal monthly payments. Since most of us operate from month to month, this is how the payments are usually made from a family budget. Is the total monthly expense something you can live with? If not, can you extend the time on major financing commitments? Can you perhaps replan a less ambitious and costly project? If you can't reduce the month-

---

Cost Estimating Checklist

Purchasing the House
☐ price of property
☐ professional inspection fee
☐ legal fees
☐ financing costs for broker's fees
☐ points of interest
☐ closing expenses for title search
☐ mortgage insurance

Restoration Costs
☐ architect's fee
☐ labor and materials
☐ construction insurance
☐ permits
☐ utilities (water, electricity, heat, during restoration)
☐ carrying costs of present home (insurance, utilities, mortgage and real estate taxes, maintaining your present home)

Operating and Maintenance Costs
☐ mortgage payments
☐ insurance
☐ taxes
☐ water
☐ sewer
☐ trash collection
☐ electricity
☐ gas & oil
☐ minor and major repairs (new roof, repainting etc.)

Total Monthly Payments _____

ly total to a livable figure, then you had better consider finding a more modest house.

Financing/Finding the Money

Once you have assembled the figures and arrived at an estimated cost for obtaining the property, restoring it, and maintaining the home, you are in a position to seek out financing for your project. Until a few years ago, funding a restoration job was a difficult task. Most lenders were not enthusiastic about investing monies in substandard neighborhoods. Fortunately, things have changed dramatically in the recent past. Things have loosened up to the point where finding the financing is not the problem. The real problem is obtaining the funds at the best possible rate.

Obtaining a mortgage at the most favorable rate is well worth the time and energy expended in the search. Saving a fraction of a percentage point over the life of a long-term loan can add up to substantial dollar savings. This is definitely a place to use all your business contacts and all the other information you have collected during the initial stages of your restoration project. Talk to anyone in the neighborhood who is familiar with the financing of a project like yours. And spend the time to shop for the best of all possible deals.

Where do you start looking for mortgage money? The traditional sources are the savings and loan associations, savings banks, some commercial banks, and FHA-approved lenders. Due to the increased attention to restoration and rehabilitation efforts by the federal government, a number of additional financing programs are available. In fact, the Department of Housing and Urban Development (HUD) has published a booklet titled *A Guide to Housing Rehabilitation Programs,* listing nearly two dozen types of federal financing programs to cover single- and multi-family projects. Then, when you add in the state programs, or the potential listing in the National Register of Historic Places with its financial benefits, you begin to understand the problem of finding the most appropriate and least expensive financing for your individual project.

Interest rates keep changing. Any figures listed here would most likely be out of date before the ink was dry. New programs are introduced and existing programs are modified or canceled. Mortgage financing is in a constant state of flux, and your wisest move is to investigate all sources fully, and take advantage of all your contacts at the time you are seeking your financing. Narrow your choice down to several lending institu-

FINANCIAL SOURCES FOR RENOVATING THE OLDER HOME:
Private Sources
Banks
Savings & Loan institutions
Neighborhood Housing Services
Foundations
Public Sources
Federal government programs
Community development block grants (HUD)
Rehabilitation loans (HUD)
Urban Homesteading Program (HUD)
State government programs
Home improvement loans for targeted areas
City government programs
Community/neighborhood programs
Historic Preservation Sources
Historic Preservation loans (under FHA Title 1)
Historic Preservation Grants-in-Aid (Dept. of Interior)

tions and apply to a number of them to discover the most advantageous terms.

When making an application, you must be prepared to submit a package of basic information. This should include a complete description of the property—exact location, size, age, condition, and an estimate of the operating costs. For rental properties, the number of apartments and anticipated income should be included.

Then a detailed list of the changes and improvements you plan as well as an estimated cost for the restoration work should be covered. Finally, a complete financial statement of your assets, income, and debts will be required. The more complete and accurate your package of information, the faster your application can be processed.

The final group of professionals you will be dealing with will all be involved in the actual restoration process. This will include any architects or structural engineers, contractors, builders or remodeling contractors, a variety of suppliers for both new and used materials, and usually, several individual craftsmen who can provide a custom touch to finish off your restoration project with a personal flair.

Photography: Karl Riek

Selecting An Architect

The right architect is the key to a successful restoration job. A competent one will usually save you more time and dollars than the fee he charges. If it is important to consider an architect in new construction, it is vital to make use of his talents when faced with a restoration job. New construction is relatively simple—things progress in an orderly, structured pattern. A restoration job, on the other hand, starts with problems, uncovers more as the work progresses, and is a constant series of surprises, disappointments, compromises, and innovative solutions. The right architect for a restoration job has both the talent and the temperament to handle the task.

The ideal individual will have had experience in previous restoration jobs in your city. The architect should be knowledgeable about the reputable contractors and various suppliers in the area. Most importantly, he should be enthusiastic about, and have complete understanding of your restoration goals. He should be part businessman, to stay within your budget, and part artist, to improve on and add to your ideas. And, since you will be spending a lot of time together, he must be an individual whose professional talents you respect as well as a person whom you feel comfortable working with.

That's a tall order, but the right architect is available if you search him out. Ask your contacts for recommendations, find out which architect was involved in restoration projects you have admired, and check with your local chapter of the American Institute of Architects for names of professionals who

More and more architects are becoming involved in restoration projects. In searching out the right one for your home, contact several, ask for their credentials, and experience and check their previous clients for a full evaluation.

specialize in restoration projects. Contact several architects, briefly explain your project, and ask for names of clients for whom they have done similar jobs.

Interview these clients and determine the architect's involvement in various stages of the project. Were his design suggestions sound and creative, did he control both the time and the cost of the restoration, did he get along with the contractor and code officials, and was he willing to listen to ideas and suggestions from the owner? Would the client recommend him for your job?

The right architect can be of assistance in the early design stages of the job or become a valuable ally for the entire term of the project. He can suggest needed repairs and detail the steps necessary for completion. His design talents can restore and improve on existing conditions, such as a more workable floor plan, which may include repositioning walls and doorways, changing the traffic patterns, or suggesting a new entrance to make the house more livable.

Depending on the size of the project and your budget, the architect can prepare the construction documents needed to obtain building permits. He can assist you in getting construction bids and selecting the contractor for the work. His knowledge of building materials and local supply sources can save many dollars. Finally, he can be your representative on the job to check on the contractor's work, coordinate with various subcontractors and building inspectors, and solve a host of unanticipated problems that arise in the course of any restoration project.

Which Contractor

Like the right architect, selecting an experienced and reliable contractor is your best insurance for a satisfactory job. Again, you or your architect must check out the reputation and background of several potential contractors, have them bid the job, and make a final selection based both on price and reputation for quality work.

A competent contractor will assume the responsibility for hiring and scheduling the work crew and supervising their efforts to assure that all work is done according to specification. He will schedule supplies and materials to make sure the right items are available for the various subcontractors to work with. In addition, he manages all the paperwork, from payrolls, social security, workman's compensation, and insurance to permits, material invoices, and coordinating building inspectors.

Because of his experience, he has a pool of construction talents and craftsmen to draw on and an on-going relationship with local suppliers that allows him to obtain materials at a professional discount. A good contractor is worth much more than just his ability to drive a nail straight.

Some individuals have chosen to act as their own general contractor, hiring individual subcontractors to work under their direction. This approach can work if you have a fairly simple restoration job, you are willing to handle all the necessary paperwork, and you have the time to be on the job at least several hours each working day. The backup of a strong architect is a virtual necessity. However, if scheduling of men and materials is not your strong talent, you are well advised to hire an experienced contractor to remove these burdens from your shoulders.

Once you have the financing and professional talent lined up, there still remains

A competent contractor, skilled in solving restoration problems, can be an excellent investment. Below, a truck-mounted crane safely places building materials on the roof during initial stages of a major restoration.

Photography: Leo Pinard

the task of locating the proper materials to complete an authentic restoration project. Today, you have a wider source of "old time" building products to choose from than at any time in the recent past. Manufacturers have rediscovered the charm and practicality of yesterday's materials and have taken positive steps to meet the growing demand for restoration products.

Restoration Suppliers

There is a growing number of national manufacturers, regional producers specializing in certain periods, and skilled craftsmen devoting their talents to providing the materials and decorative elements needed for historically correct restoration projects.

Take a relatively simple item like paint, for instance. Our ancestors had a surprisingly colorful eye when it came to decorating the exterior and interior of their homes. America's recent Bicentennial celebration, and the burgeoning interest in historical restoration, have spawned a revival in the man-

Tremont Nail Company, Wareham, Massachusetts, founded in 1819, is America's oldest nail manufacturer. The company offers the traditional patterns of cut nails appropriate to the period of restoration being undertaken. In addition to a variety of nail styles and suggested decorative applications, they provide information to help a restorer determine the authenticity and age of a structure based on nail examination. Nail types and ideas are illustrated below.

ufacture of traditional colors. Sherwin Williams Co., Cleveland, Ohio, has developed, after careful research, a series of "Heritage Color Palettes." Each series of color-combinations is keyed to the architecture and feeling of a distinct section of our country. The Pennsylvania Dutch palette includes slate gray, Dutch blue, and barn red, while the Western Ranch palette covers desert gold, trail brown, cactus green, and sagebrush gray. Pittsburgh Paints has taken a similar approach, from Newport brown, Appalachian fern, and Salem green to Arizona clay, Amish blue, and Colorado sandstone. Don't be misled by the colorful regional names. These colors represent much more than names on paint can labels. The manufacturers have delved deeply into the past and compiled accurate colors, then taken the added step to produce pamphlets and books to assist the homeowner in creating authentic color schemes.

The Tremont Nail Co. continues to operate one of the earliest nail factories founded in 1819 at Wareham, Massachusetts. They specialize in old-fashioned cut nails and are one of the few manufacturers still shipping their product in the traditional 100-pound wooden kegs. Interestingly, the square-cut tapered nails have 70 percent more holding power than the typical wire nails used today. The company produces a variety of sizes and lengths for flooring, shingle, slate, sheathing, and boat applications. Decorative wrought

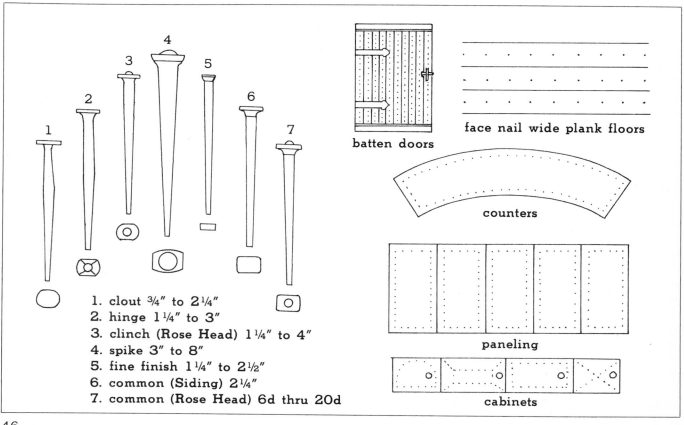

1. clout ¾" to 2¼"
2. hinge 1¼" to 3"
3. clinch (Rose Head) 1¼" to 4"
4. spike 3" to 8"
5. fine finish 1¼" to 2½"
6. common (Siding) 2¼"
7. common (Rose Head) 6d thru 20d

batten doors

face nail wide plank floors

counters

paneling

cabinets

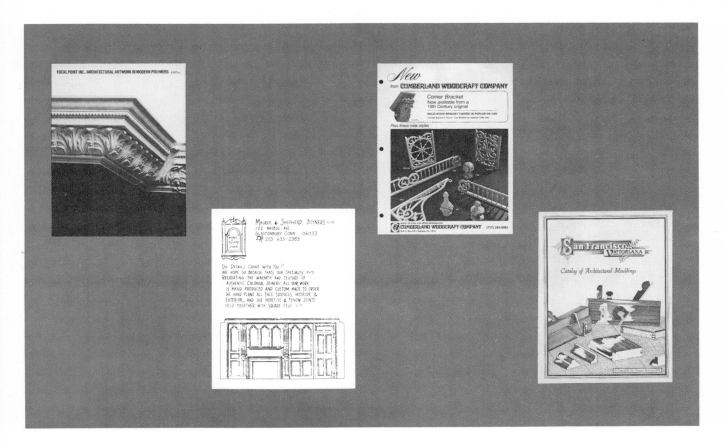

head designs for restoration work include clout, hinge, clinch, spike, finish, wrought, and rose head patterns.

Tremont Nail Co. not only supplies the restoration market but they are an integral part of the movement. In 1976, the Tremont Nail Factory District was included in the National Register of Historic Places.

Many millwork houses are blowing the dust off long-stored moulding knives to recreate the traditional millwork patterns. E.A. Nord Company, Everett, Washington, took part in the restoration of the Wait House, built in 1899, in Little Rock, Arkansas (see pages 50-51). During an earlier modernization, the wood columns and turnings around the porch were replaced with wrought iron. As part of the recent restoration, the home was restored to its original Victorian styling by using tapered wood columns and turned spindles on the main porch.

Focal Point, Inc., of Marietta, Georgia, reproduces the ornate look of plaster ceiling medallions, cornice mouldings, stair brackets, and fireplace mantels. A number of architectural styles from Old English to Georgian and French Provincial are in their catalog.

In the East, Mauer and Shepard, Joyners, Glastonbury, Connecticut, creates customized authentic colonial millwork, carved doors, peg-jointed wood windows, mouldings in the traditional patterns, and other decorative and structural wood parts.

Increasing interest in restoration activity has spawned a host of new companies reviving older patterns and materials. Above a collection of catalogs offering everything from stamped tin ceilings to traditional millwork profiles.

At Williamsburg, Virginia, the site of what is probably the best-known American restoration community, a number of manufacturers have been licensed by the Colonial Williamsburg Foundation to reproduce exact copies of hardware, fabrics, wallpaper, furniture, lighting fixtures, and paint colors. Until 1780, when the capital was moved to Richmond, Williamsburg was the political center of Britain's largest colony in North America. In 1926, John D. Rockefeller, Jr., established the foundation which has restored approximately 90 original structures including residences, public buildings and shops.

In Colorado, the Silverton Victorian Mill Works recreates custom woodwork in oak, redwood, and pine. Much of their production is moulding, with over three dozen patterns of door and window casings. In addition, corner and base blocks, decorative brackets, paneled wainscoting, siding patterns, paneled entrance doors, window sash, and even wood storm window kits are manufactured. Although the company name indicates a strength in Victorian patterns, many of the wide baseboard and casing mouldings, siding and wainscot patterns, and ceiling cornice mouldings conform to traditional colonial configurations.

San Francisco has been called "the wooden city" because of the unusual architectural use of the abundant supply of redwood in northern California. Victorian styling, popular in homes built between 1865 and 1910, account for some 50,000 homes in San Francisco alone.

To counter the trend for stripping off the gingerbread and other embellishments for the sake of modernization, a small group of dedicated craftsmen founded San Francisco Victoriana in 1972. To stop the plunder and restore the Victorian architectural heritage, the group offers advice based on their extensive research, as well as authentically styled wood and plaster mouldings, reproduction and antique lighting fixtures, wallpaper, borders, period hardware, and ceramic pulls. Their millwork shop reproduces newels, finials, turnings, ornate fretwork, doors, and decorative shingles and siding.

Before ordering any newly produced period building materials, you should consider checking into the salvage and wrecking yards in your area. Here, savings can be substantial compared to the cost of new materials. For instance, you may be able to find a salvaged paneled door for $10 or $20 compared to several hundred dollars for a brand new one.

According to Engineering News Record's annual survey of specialty contractors, the largest wrecking organization in the country is Cleveland Wrecking Company of Los Angeles with offices in Cincinnati, Philadelphia, New York, Chicago, and San Francisco. The $35 million firm began in 1910 when the five Rose brothers of Minneapolis organized the company naming it after their Ohio hometown. Although primarily involved in commercial demolition, Cleveland Wrecking boasts that they will tackle anything from a skyscraper to a chicken coop.

A number of smaller salvage operations are filling the gap between the large commercial wrecking companies and the local antique dealers. United House Wrecking, Stamford, Connecticut, with six acres of rough timbers, stained glass windows, hundreds of doors, plumbing and electrical fixtures, and other period furnishings, bills itself as "the Junkyard with Personality." Other yards have equally colorful names—Materials Unlimited, Ypsilanti, Michigan; Olde Theatre

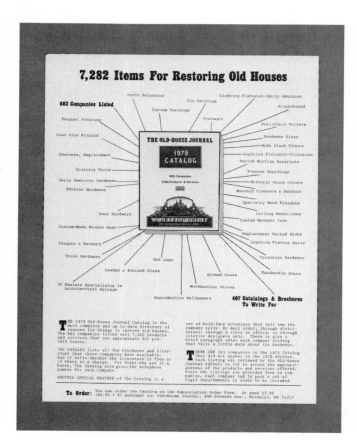

An annual directory from the "Old House Journal," the catalog lists 7,282 items for restoring old houses. The products and services offered in the Buyer's Guide are appropriate for pre-1920 houses.

The United House Wrecking Company is just one of the many "junkyards" that can be found throughout the country, specializing in antiques and hard to find items for restoration projects.

48

Architectural Salvage Co., Kansas City; The Wrecking Bar, Dallas; Urban Archaeology Ltd., New York; The Second Chance, Macon, Georgia; and Rejuvenation House Parts Co., Portland, Oregon.

When shopping at wrecking and salvage yards, you must know what you are looking for and carry with you accurate information as to sizes, species, and styles. With a little luck and perseverance you can obtain both structural and decorative elements at substantial bargains. Check your Yellow Page listings under headings such as Building Materials, Used, House Wreckers, Demolition, Salvage, and Wrecking Yards.

Two annual directories that list sources for both new and used building materials, fixtures and decorative elements are the *Sourcebook* published by the Early American Society and *Buyer's Guide* from The Old House Journal. Both publications offer a wealth of information and contacts to help you when searching out those hard-to-find items needed to complete your restoration.

The final category of suppliers is the local individual or small custom shop, which specializes in designing and producing period items to your specifications. It might be a custom stained glass window, hand-carved fireplace mantel, tile or brick work, or hand-forged hardware or grillework. If you are looking for custom millwork or woodturnings, you don't need a carpenter or even a craftsman—you are looking for an artisan who can design as well as produce a special item to fit your needs.

Richard D. Scofield, founder of Period Lighting Fixtures, Chester, Connecticut, is fairly typical of the new breed of artisan. After completing his education, he "retired" for several years and toured Sweden. There, in order to earn enough to support his travels, he found work by chance with a local crafstman producing custom ornamental iron works. Here, he rediscovered his attraction to hand craftsmanship. As a member of an old New England family, his grandfather was a naval architect and it was only natural that Scofield, along with his father and brother, spent many hours building and maintaining a series of boats. When he returned to the United States, he apprenticed himself to "an excellent but ornery" old New England craftsman creating custom lighting fixtures. After two years, he left. "The timing was right," he said. "It was a combination of low wages, a personality conflict with the boss, and the fact that I had learned all that I could."

He opened his own shop, and today produces a series of carefully researched lighting

Photography: Period Lighting Fixtures

Richard Scofield, founder of Period Lighting Fixtures, Chester, Connecticut, patiently handcrafts a small colonial chandelier. Workshop wall displays variety of authentically styled copper and pewter wall sconces.

fixture designs based on historical archives records, museums and restoration villages. The interior chandeliers and sconces are pewter, aged or painted tin while the exterior wall and post lanterns are made of natural copper, painted flat black or oxidized to produce an aged green patina.

Scofield concentrates on 17th- and 18th-century lighting fixtures since, as he explains, "After that period, much of the hand craftsmanship was lost to mass production." And authenticity is important, right down to the traditional crossbar arms on his lantern posts, which were used long ago by the city lamplighter to prop his short ladder against as he nightly lit each of the town's lanterns.

49

Chapter 4
Avoiding Restoration Mistakes

ow that you've found and acquired that older home, completed enough research to convince yourself that you have a diamond in the rough and lined up the qualified professional assistance to do the proper restoration job, are you ready to begin? Not just yet.

Although you are anxious to show some immediate progress, contain your enthusiasm and take a deep breath. Any successful restoration project is a series of carefully planned and executed detail operations. Each must be done correctly and it is important that all steps be taken in the right sequence to avoid costly and time-consuming mistakes. No restoration job ever seems to have enough dollars and hours, so any initial steps you can take to conserve either will be a good investment.

No professional diamond cutter, no matter how experienced, ever slices into a raw stone of value without devoting weeks or months to a careful analysis of the task. He realizes that once he reaches for the cleaver and mallet to strike the initial blow, he is committed. Once he begins, there is no turning back for a fresh start. Your diamond in the rough deserves the same careful consideration. It may have stood for decades or generations so a few more hours devoted to avoiding serious mistakes is time well spent.

The object of your preliminary planning is to avoid any sweeping corrections. If you can anticipate problems, you then can often eliminate or solve them before they create a serious stumbling block.

General Approach

The thinking is basic: (A) analyze the job completely, (B) estimate the dollars, time and energy needed, and (C) plan your attack in a logical step-by-step manner.

The detailed notes you made during the initial house inspection and any later professional inspections are a good starting point for your restoration analysis. What are the major structural problems that must be corrected? What mechanical improvements are required to put the home in a livable condition for your family? Plumbing? Heating system? Electrical? Insulation?

In addition, will you be making changes in the floor plan to improve traffic flow, guarantee privacy, or possibly finish off or subdivide existing space to create new rooms? What about storage? Is there enough in the right locations or will you need to create new closets, build in additional drawers and cabinets? Can the old pantry off the kitchen be converted into a laundry room or your private wine cellar? What about a new family room, workshop, or sewing center? Get all your ideas and desires down on paper. Then go back and review the list putting priorities on each item. Be realistic. Group your individual ideas into "must do," "would like to do," and "gee, I hope we can eventually do," categories. These are not always easy decisions but with some honest discussion and a

Thanks to old photos in the historical archives, a period home in Little Rock, Arkansas, was easily restored without producing any style errors. The before picture at the left shows wrought iron columns and railings which had been added by an earlier owner. The completed restoration at the far left includes replacement wood columns, turned wood railing, a new roof and railings on the roof walk area.

Photography: E.A. Nord Company

Photography: Colonial Williamsburg

Recreating a traditional period garden can be an exciting and satisfying part of any restoration project. The Curtis-Maupin garden (bottom photo), in Colonial Williamsburg, features clipped dwarf boxwood hedging in triangular patterns. The Bryan house garden (upper photo) provides a honeysuckle-covered arbor for a cool resting place in summer. The arbor overlooks parterres of clipped box and both standard and dwarf fruit trees.

little give and take among family members, you can reach agreement in most of the important areas.

There are several additional decisions concerning the appearance of the completed project which must be made early in your final analysis. Create the finished restoration in your mind. Mentally make the repairs and envision how the landscaping will set off the exterior details. Picture guests arriving at your front door and being ushered into your living room to warm themselves before your handsome fireplace. How will the candlelight reflect off the pictures and silverware during a formal dinner?

Then consider the day-to-day activities — the late Sunday morning breakfast, the birthday parties and private quiet hours, the ordi-

nary cooking, cleaning, and general household tasks that bind any family closer to their home. Fix the complete picture in your mind.

Refer to your historical research notes to settle one major question. Just what period in the life of your house will you recreate? Perhaps you will decide to restore the house to its original splendor—to reproduce that moment in history when the builder first turned over the keys to the new owner.

On the other hand, oldest is not always best. For instance, you may have discovered that your home was built in 1890 and was substantially remodeled in 1916 by a prominent businessman of the community who later made a name for himself in local politics. The combination of the structural improvements and historical prominence of the later family may suggest that a 1916 restoration might be more satisfactory. The decision is yours, but some specific date must be established toward which your restoration activities are pointed. Without some unifying theme, it is surprisingly easy to drift into an architectural hodgepodge where the roof treatment conflicts with the siding material and the door style contradicts the handle and hinge design. It's like living in a permanent garage sale—a lot more confusing than interesting.

Another major decision must be made early in your analysis. Just how authentic are you willing to make your restoration? Personal taste as well as practicality plays a big part in establishing your restoration accuracy. Just how pure can you afford to be? With enough effort you can accurately recreate a period home right down to the last detail, but most families are not comfortable living in a "museum" atmosphere. Most are willing to forgo the adventures of outdoor plumbing for more modern and efficient fixtures. Shoveling coal into and cleaning ash and clinkers out of an old furnace never was much fun even in the good old days, so a modern heating plant makes more sense.

It is often possible to modernize original elements in an older home to make them more efficient without completely destroying their charm. Old gas light fixtures can usually be rewired for electrical bulbs. Paint-covered hardware or heater grilles can be stripped, polished, or replated to restore their original luster.

Mechanical systems and equipment present more of a challenge. Old steam heat radiators can be made operable, but even in good working condition, they do not represent the most efficient method of heating your home today. You can still find someone willing to deliver huge blocks of ice to cool

Dramatic before and after photos, above, illustrate the impact of a sound restoration procedure. The original house had been completely stripped of any personality. Yet, with the help of San Francisco Victoriana, proper research was conducted, the facade totally rebuilt with redwood decorative parts, and a contrasting paint job carefully planned to showcase the architectural detailing to best advantage.

your brass-bound oak ice chest, but carrying sloshing pans of melted ice water is a hazardous chore at best.

And what about those modern time-savers in the kitchen? No housewife exposed to the wonders of a garbage disposal, automatic dishwasher, indoor grill, and microwave oven is usually willing to take a step back in time. The old black cast-iron stove dominating the kitchen with its ruddy glow is pure nostalgia. However, starting a fire or banking the coals everytime you want a hot cup of coffee doesn't appeal to today's busy woman. If you are going to reproduce a large colonial farmhouse or Victorian mansion, are you willing to reproduce the large staff of maids, cooks, and handymen needed to make it operate properly? If not, then you are faced with some compromises.

Compromise Approaches

How have other families handled the question of compromising authentic restoration in their own projects? Some have accepted no compromise whatsoever. Their restoration results in a pure reconstruction of a period home from the rebuilding and repair right down to the bull's-eye glass above the front door and hand-forged nails in the flooring. The interior design, fixtures, and furnishings reflect the time and attention payed to searching out the right antiques, locating salvage parts and hardware or finding authentic reproductions of materials, furniture,

Interior restoration can follow traditional concepts as shown in the top photo above. This small home in Granville, Ohio, relied on period wallpaper and furnishings to reproduce a charming Midwestern farmhouse atmosphere. Below, a different approach was taken by using more contemporary furnishings and a sculptured floor rug to contrast and highlight the handsome fireplace, columns and ornate millwork.

and accessories to complete the job. The project may take years and is expensive, but it can be done. For some, this museum-like atmosphere is totally pleasing and well worth the effort and expense. This "no compromise" approach is usually taken by those restorers with more time and money and fewer young children.

Most restorations are a compromise, and with good reason. Not all of the original building materials are easily obtainable. A slate roof may last for centuries, but making major repairs today can be a real problem. The slate itself may not be available, and even if you can locate the material, you're

Photography: Karl Riek

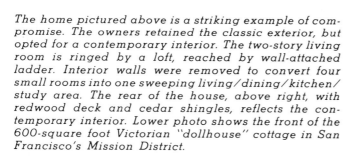

The home pictured above is a striking example of compromise. The owners retained the classic exterior, but opted for a contemporary interior. The two-story living room is ringed by a loft, reached by wall-attached ladder. Interior walls were removed to convert four small rooms into one sweeping living/dining/kitchen/study area. The rear of the house, above right, with redwood deck and cedar shingles, reflects the contemporary interior. Lower photo shows the front of the 600-square foot Victorian "dollhouse" cottage in San Francisco's Mission District.

faced with the problem of where to find the skilled labor to apply it. The art of splitting slate, creating nail holes, and hanging a slate roof with copper valleys and flashing is dying. Early wood parts and millwork were often custom-produced, the same craftsman using the same tools sometimes never duplicated the same house twice. Even early factory-made window sash, siding, mouldings, and stairways employed patterns which are no longer produced. A few of the early designs, particularly the colonial and Victorian patterns, are being reproduced by younger craftsmen, but much of the rich architectural detailing has been lost.

With a sufficiently large budget custom parts can be recreated. However, the process is time-consuming and expensive. To make repairs on a wood staircase, for instance,

may require: (1) finding a machinist to custom-grind shaper knives or hand scrapers for reproducing the rail, (2) locating a millwork house or cabinetmaker to produce the hand rail, (3) engaging a wood turner to produce newell posts and balusters, and (4) finding a competent refinisher who can match the replacement parts to the original material. With luck, you may find several of these talents under one roof, but in most cases you'll end up dealing with four separate individuals.

Practicality and personal taste indicate areas where compromises can be made. One family, in restoring an urban townhouse, analyzed the exterior and decided to leave things pretty much as they were. Their research indicated the original exterior had been remodeled years earlier and now matched the surrounding homes. Since their home had no outstanding architectural features, they felt no compelling need to recreate the original look or feel of the earlier design. Instead, a badly needed roof was added, ordinary exterior maintenance performed, and a fresh coat of paint applied.

As part of their compromise, they decided to concentrate their efforts and dollars on the interior. Here, a real transformation took place. Layers of paint and wallpaper were stripped, floors sanded and refinished, walls and ceilings repaired. The children helped to strip and refinish hardware items, carry tools and materials to the work areas, and assist in the cleanup projects. For a "vacation" from their labors, the family haunted garage sales, second-hand shops, and estate sales. The result was an accurate and comfortable interior that captured the charm of an earlier era.

In contrast, a young Mid-Western couple took a different approach to their classic Carpenter Gothic house. This was an architectural gem replete with gingerbread woodwork, ornate front porch, and fancy columns and railings. Broken pieces were carefully repaired, missing elements created and replaced, then the exterior received a multicolor paint job to highlight the various architectural details. To showcase this home, the setting was framed in an ornate picket fence surrounding the property. Shade trees plus carefully selected flowers and shrubs flanking the walk completed the picture.

The interior, however, presented an entirely different atmosphere. Stark white walls and ceilings set off several handsome pieces of period furniture but the majority of the furnishings were decidedly modern. Bright metals, shag rugs, modern leather sofa, and contemporary artwork throughout. The net effect was tasteful and comfortable but in direct contrast to the exterior. Yet somehow it was perfect for this particular couple.

In working out your personal compromise between authenticity and practicality, it does not have to be a black or white choice. Compromise, by its nature, is a degree decision. You can lean toward either extreme or establish a more comfortable stance someplace in the middle. Time may play an important part in your ultimate decision. You may not be able to complete your dream restoration in six months. Insufficient money to hire the army of professional help needed for a quick completion and lack of time on your part to make all the decisions, find the right craftsmen, materials, and accessories, make a six-month project impossible. But before you concede too many compromises, try extending the time frame. What could you

Photography: Steve Hogben

In another compromise approach, a tiny Carpenter Gothic home in Atlanta, Georgia features a stained glass window in the front parlor. Salvaged window is mounted on large screw eyes in front of the existing double-hung window. Open plan living room, in center photo, combines traditional mantel and furniture with contemporary splashes of color. Exterior view, below, shows retained gingerbread trim, and unusual, original herringbone patterned facade.

Photography: Leo Pinard

Serious foundation problems are not usually a repair job for the average homeowner. Major structural work should be completed first before any exterior or interior decorative repairs are begun. Above, sagging support beams have been jacked into level position, then wood foundation forms assembled and braced carefully. The final step will require pouring a new concrete foundation wall and lowering the house frame into position.

do if the restoration took place over two years or six years rather than six months? More time would certainly help the financial situation and give you the opportunity to do more yourself and rely less on expensive professional labor. Time can be your ally. Plan to use it to your advantage.

To avoid restoration mistakes, you need a well-thought-out plan of attack. Without a systematic approach to restoration, you will find yourself constantly running from one emergency to another, have too much material underfoot causing confusion or be missing critical supplies to keep your crew working. You also run the very real risk of creating serious and unnecessary problems for yourself. There is nothing more disheartening than undoing something you have just completed. Knocking apart a freshly plastered wall to repair faulty wiring can be expensive. Watching stains collect on the new ceiling the first time it rains through the leaky roof is an exercise in frustration. Repairs must be made in an orderly manner or they may be self-defeating.

Restoration Plan

The business world has a saying that applies with equal validity to the world of restoration. "Plan your work and work your plan." The idea sounds logical and simple to follow but a restoration project is latent with surprises. Hidden problems surface or unusual opportunities are uncovered. Both can raise havoc with a reconstruction schedule. Whatever the emergency, you at least have a plan to deviate from and return to.

Since each restoration project is unique, there is no one plan that fits every job. The plan, to be successful, must conform to the individual circumstances. However, every plan is based on a series of proven principles. In general, you will avoid costly mistakes if you work from the outside toward the inside, progress from the top downward, and move from structural toward decorative.

There are two critical areas that must be taken care of simultaneously. The home must be made weathertight and any structural foundation repairs completed before any other restoration work proceeds. Water and excessive moisture can be a restorer's biggest enemy. A leaking roof must be patched or completely reroofed. Gutters and downspouts must be repaired or replaced so that rain runs off the roof and is led away from the foundation. There is no sense in attempting any interior work that may later be ruined by a leaking roof or storing materials in a basement that is flooded by the first rain.

Missing or broken siding should be fixed to prevent any further water damage to wall interiors. Broken windows should be reglazed or at least boarded over temporarily to defeat the weather and eliminate vandalism. Leaking basement walls should be sealed and a sump pump and dehumidifying equipment installed to assure a moisture-free basement.

Severely damaged foundations or badly rotted and termite infested wooden sill plates must be corrected. Major structural problems of this nature often require jacking up portions of the house off the foundation so repair work can be performed. Even the most careful workmen, when jacking up a house, run the risk of cracking plaster walls and forcing window and door frames out of square. Obviously, foundation problems should be solved before other repairs are attempted.

Next, you should consider making all mechanical repairs to the heating, plumbing, and electrical systems. What is the proper sequence? Common sense will usually dictate the answer. If your home is in the northern climates and the work is being done during the winter, the heating system, to prevent you, the workmen, and your pipes from freezing, might be the first task. However, if your wiring is badly frayed and presents a fire hazard or if the system is inadequately powered so fuses are constantly being blown, then the electrical circuits should get prime attention. On the other hand, if you intend to live in the house while the restoration work takes place, then at least one working bathroom takes on significant importance and priority.

You can best determine your own schedule for mechanical repairs. In rewiring and adding additional electrical circuits, replacing piping and repositioning plumbing fixtures, and installing a new heater or air conditioning system with ductwork, vents, and controls, some damage to walls and floors is bound to occur. This is the reason these mechanical improvements should be completed before any finish work is started.

The same reasoning holds true for adding insulation. Whether you use rolled, loose, or foam material, insulating a home is a messy job. It may be necessary to rip up attic floorboards to insulate the upper story. Wall insulation usually requires holes be drilled through the top plate or through the upper wall from the inside or outside, inserting a large hose, and blowing loose insulation or foam into each stud cavity.

The remaining work falls into a logical pattern depending on weather conditions and your personal preferences. But keep in mind the general rules of proceeding from the structural to the decorative and working from the top down. For instance, you might want to take advantage of good weather and tackle the exterior projects first. Make chimney, roofing, gutter, and downspout repairs. Then attack wood siding, trim boards, and any missing parts. Next, windows, doors, porch columns, railings, decks, and stairs. Once all repairs and replacements are made, painting is the final step. Start at the top and work down. If you start at the bottom first, you will inevitably end up with ladder marks and paint drips from the fascia and roof trim on your freshly painted siding. Avoid problems by working in the right sequence.

Detached buildings, such as garage or storage sheds, fencing, gardens, and other landscaping are usually left until the interior work is completed.

Inside, the first rule is one of safety. Make sure loose stairs and railings are repaired and there is adequate lighting on stairways and other traffic areas. Usually, the kitchen and bath are the first rooms that receive attention. You may not want to completely finish them at this time but at least put them in reasonable working order. Then, depending on your family, you may want to proceed to the living room, dining room, and halls before you work on the bedrooms. Or perhaps the family room comes first, then the sleeping areas and more public rooms.

You might start the interior work by removing all unnecessary doors. Demount them from the hinges and set them aside. This allows easier access as you move materials from room to room and prevents the doors from being damaged. If you plan to refinish the doors, now is the time to strip off the hardware, chip off layers of paint, and polish the metal parts. A thin coat of clear lacquer spray will protect the shine. Consider having the doors stripped by a commercial organization. They have the equipment to dip full-size doors into tanks of remover. For a few dollars cost per door, you

*Before picture shows the 117-year-old house in Dorchester, Massachusetts, bought by station **WGBH** of Boston as the subject for their 13-week restoration series, "This Old House." Badly neglected but still sound.*

The ramshackle single-family home received a new roof, shutters and a fresh coat of paint. Porch with turned columns, picket fence, and a badly overdue landscaping project completed the transformation.

Photography: WGBH, Boston

can save yourself hours of messy hand stripping and scraping.

Ceiling work should be done first, then wall repairs and finally, the floors. You may want to work room by room or complete one house level at a time. Your decision will largely depend on whether you are living in the house during restoration and must maintain access to certain rooms, or if the entire project can be worked on while you take up residence elsewhere.

Before You Begin

Enthusiasm can be the restorer's biggest problem. In the rush to get the job underway, important historical evidence is often removed or destroyed. Before you pick up the first hammer or turn the contractor and his crew loose, stop for a final look around the property. This is particularly necessary if the home has not been lived in for some time.

The natural tendency is to do a quick cleanup, dispose of the rubble and junk, then get on with the restoration work. Unfortunately, during the cleanup stage, vital historic information may be destroyed or disposed of by an enthusiastic amateur. When removing underbrush, weeds, and shrubs from around the foundation, carefully sort out and examine any foreign objects. Broken hardware and derelict materials from the original building may hold important clues. You may uncover evidence of old walkways, remains of foundations, flower and garden beds, or even salvageable plants and shrubs. Shards of glass or a buried flat stone by the foundation wall may indicate where original windows or doors were located before they were sided over.

Junk in the basement, garage, or sheds deserves careful inspection before it is discarded. With luck, you can discover a treasure of old shutters, window sash, doors, boxes of plumbing and lighting fixtures, door handles and hinges. Much of the material may still be usable, supply spare parts for repair work or at least provide clues for replacement pieces. Check into all the dark corners, in the crawl spaces of partial basements and in the attic under the eaves. As you go, take note of any construction details in unfinished or exposed areas. Many times you will find original roof shingles or pieces of beveled siding used as wedges to level a floor above a basement beam or to shim out a window or door frame. Any house is full of historical clues if you search knowingly.

Your inspection may uncover a treasure of building materials in some unlikely locations. Old time carpenters, like their modern counterparts, often used surplus materials to finish off sections of a house. One family in Illinois salvaged more than enough material to replace deteriorated exterior siding. The old coal bin, tucked behind the furnace in the basement, was built with clear beveled siding boards. In Connecticut, left-over hardwood lumber paneling from the dining room was used as shelving in the pantry off the kitchen. Beside a St. Louis garage, an early homeowner had built a cold frame from original windows in the home to start his spring plants. Unfortunately, the long outside exposure to the elements had pretty much rotted the wood sash, but enough was left to determine the window size and construction, plus the old wavy glass panes were saved as replacements for the reconstructed windows.

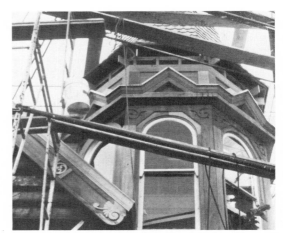

Photography: From the archives of San Francisco Victoriana

Restoration Sequence

General approach:
A. Work from the outside toward the inside of the home.

B. Start from the top and work down.

C. Move from structural repairs toward the decorative. Avoid serious and costly mistakes by working in a logical sequence, completing each segment before moving on to the next major project:
1. Make the exterior weathertight.
2. Complete all major foundation repairs.
3. Mechanical elements — heating, plumbing, electrical.
4. Install necessary insulation.
5. Complete all exterior and interior repairs before starting any finish work.

Old moulding sections were often used for shelf cleats in walk-in closets, pantries, and storage areas. Extra baseboard or door casing moulding may have been used on the wall for hook strips or clothes peg supports. Attic floors traditionally absorbed the surplus roofing, siding, or floorboards from other sections of the house. One restorer, working on an Ohio farmhouse, literally found a gold mine in his attic. While moving out old cartons from the dusty attic, he noticed that the thick floorboards were not nailed in place but had been laid loosely across the floor joist. On closer inspection, he discovered the rough, wide boards were clear walnut lumber. A local furniture manufacturer eagerly paid several thousand dollars for this prime growth walnut, which had been seasoning for more than 80 years.

Additional sources of authentic building materials may not be quite so obvious. You can usually salvage parts from little used or inconspicuous locations throughout the house. This "cannibalizing" technique is usually the best and least expensive method to obtain small quantities of key millwork parts that are no longer produced commercially. As long as you conduct the salvage work with an eye toward the overall restoration plan, stealing parts from one section of the house to use in more prominent areas makes good sense.

An unfinished attic, for instance, is probably the least important segment of restoring a house. Here, you may be able to strip door casing and baseboard mouldings, door hardware, and other items from the attic side. Use the material to replace missing parts from the main floor and no one will ever discover your creative thievery in the attic.

Finish moulding can usually be stripped from the inside of large closets and walk-in pantries where the loss will be unnoticed. Salvaging mouldings requires a gentle touch to prevent damage to old, dry wood parts. Start by using a sharp knife to break any paint seal between the piece to be removed and the remaining woodwork. Then slip a broad blade putty knife into the joint and gently pry apart the sections. Stubborn mouldings may need a wide chisel or pry bar to force the section from the wall but leave the putty knife in place to protect the plaster or wallpaper from damage.

Most moulding was applied with small-headed finish nails rather than the larger, flat-headed common nails used in general construction. If you try to bang the nails out from the back of the moulding, you will inevitably split out the face of the moulding where the nail head comes through. A better method is to remove the finish nails through the back of the wood. Sometimes a standard claw hammer can do the job. Other times, a pair of pliers or a nail-nipper will be needed to secure a grip on the nail shank. Pulling nails through the back of the moulding leaves the face smooth and splinter free.

Final Preliminary Step

By this time, you should be familiar with the house and know what you hope the final restoration will look like. Major problem areas have been identified, final design changes approved, financing and professional help arranged, and the plan of attack defined. Before the workmen swarm over the project, draw up a detailed list of specific do's and don'ts, warnings and requests covering each area of the restoration project.

Your list should fully explain and identify what portions are to be repaired or replaced and where the matching material will come from. For instance, "All wood siding that is cupped or loose will be nailed flat with 8d finish nails, cracked and split siding to be repaired with exterior glue, missing siding boards to be salvaged from the back side of garage." Or, "All wallpaper in upstairs hall and bedrooms to be removed but wallpaper

Often old mouldings can be salvaged from inconspicuous areas and used in restoring more prominent sections of a house. Check a finished attic, pantry or large walk-in closets for out-of-production wood patterns. Since old mouldings may be brittle with age, they must be stripped carefully. Use a standard claw hammer, working as close to the nails as possible. A wide putty knife will adequately protect the plaster. Start at one end of the moulding and then pry gently.

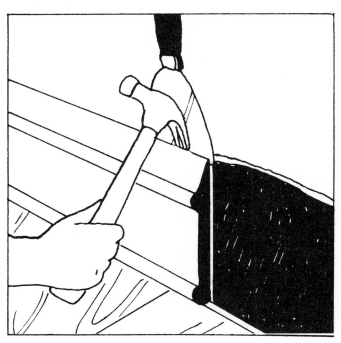

in living and dining rooms to be retained. No damage, fingerprints, or pencil notations — PLEASE."

Workmen are human and, like anyone else, will take the easiest and quickest way to complete a job. However, you must explain in detail each step of the restoration process. Carefully define all items that will be removed and how the demolition is to be done. Then, make a similar list of those parts to be added to the project. "All asbestos siding and furring strips to be removed from exterior walls down to original clapboard siding. Dispose of all asbestos and any furring strips on west wall of garage." Or, "Main stairway to be carefully disassembled, stripped, reassembled with replacement for missing balusters, and refinished. Save all broken and splintered stairway parts for possible repair." Or, "New 3-0 wide doorway to kitchen cut through east wall of dining room (see floor plan for exact location). Dispose of all wallpaper and plaster from cut-out. Salvage lath for use in repairing water damaged wall in upstairs back bedroom." In each case, be specific as to what must be done, how it

should be done, and what is the disposition of the material.

Your list should include a request that any workman discovering extra building materials, unusual construction, or any objects of historical interest should notify you or the job superintendent immediately. While removing paneling or stripping moulding or wallpaper, layers of original paint or wallcoverings may be revealed. Sometimes this new information comes as a surprise and that is part of the excitement and challenge of a restoration project. The new information may modify your original plans but make sure that all the workmen know you are interested in anything unusual before they plow ahead and destroy the evidence.

At the same time, clearly define what part you intend to play in the total project. Will you work along with the crew in the hauling and scraping or do they operate on their own? Do they clean up the work area daily (at a fairly healthy cost per hour) or will you and your family be responsible for the clean-up task? If you accept the job, be sure to follow through on schedule. You can avoid a

Another method of obtaining an accurate moulding profile is to remove a heating grille, and trace the exposed moulding end.

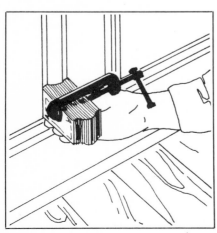

You can make a workable contour gauge by pushing several loosely clamped decks of cards against the profile.

Contour gauge, with sliding metal fingers, is used to duplicate the profile of ornate moulding patterns when traced on paper.

lot of misunderstandings if all parties know the extent and limitations of their jobs.

Make your list as complete as possible and in the general sequence of your restoration plan. Much of the physical improvements and changes will be spelled out on the architect's blueprints but your detailed list will answer many of the day-to-day questions. If the architect is responsible for job supervision, be sure to review your detailed list with him. Post the list in a conspicuous location on the job and spend a few minutes with the contractor and his crew explaining the details. Establish one individual—the architect, contractor, or yourself—as the one to make all final decisions. Conflicting information and countermanding orders on any job lead to total confusion. One and only one individual must have final responsibility.

The ideal time to put together your shopping list for replacement parts is after your list of repair and replacement details is assembled and before construction begins.

If possible, salvage a small piece of siding or moulding to use when looking for new material at the building material center or lumberyard. Remove a window sash or door knob when shopping for replacements at a wrecking yard or salvage store. If it is impossible to remove a hand sample or if the object is too bulky, a paneled door for instance, make a rough sketch of the general design, take specific measurements of width, height, thickness, notes on the type of material, decorative details, finish, and other important points. To duplicate the profile of complicated moulding patterns, you can often slip a piece of paper into a crack or opening and trace the profile from the original material onto the paper. Removing a baseboard heating grille will usually expose the adjacent moulding profile.

Broken or missing exterior decorative and trim parts can be duplicated easily in most cases if you use one of the remaining sound parts as a model or pattern. Sometimes it is easier to duplicate an ornate pattern on paper by using an inexpensive contour gauge. The gauge is nothing more than a simple clamp or framework holding a series of short wire lengths. The individual steel "fingers" slide within the holder. To duplicate an exact profile, the fingers are gently pushed against the moulding until they conform to the design. You can then trace the profile edge from the gauge onto a piece of paper and take this with you to compare available moulding patterns at the lumber yard or salvage operation. Take the time to make your shopping list as detailed and as accurate as possible.

Typical Restoration Mistakes

Any restoration project provides the opportunity for a variety of mistakes. However, most mistakes are neither financial nor of the structural kind. If you are a reasonably sane individual, have heeded the advice of a knowledgeable real estate professional, and have followed the counsel of your local banker, then you can't get hurt too badly. You were probably able to buy the property at a good and fair market value. With the improvements you plan to make and the constantly rising real estate market, you should be relatively safe. The project may cost 20 percent more and take 50 percent longer to complete than originally estimated but if you went in with your eyes open, then this may be no real surprise. However, if your rich uncle just died and you insist on dropping $300,000 into your restoration project when the surrounding homes are valued at $50,000—well, there are worse ways of squandering your inheritance.

Structurally, no beginning architect or contractor with any professional pride will allow you to get into serious trouble. If, for some reason, you forgo the use of these professional talents, then you still must hurdle the building inspector. Before approving your work, the inspector will assure you that the roof won't fall, the wiring won't start a fire, and the furnace won't explode the first time you fire it up. Structurally, the job will be safe.

If any mistakes are to be made, they will most likely occur in the area of aesthetics. At best, you will have completed a restoration job you can be proud of. At worst, you will have just another residential remodeling job to talk about.

There are some general guidelines that will assist you in completing a successful restoration project:

1. **Do your homework**. It's vital that you have taken the time to fully research the individual history of the house itself, familiarized yourself with the surrounding neighborhood and gained a comfortable knowledge of the style house you are restoring.

Analyze your family's needs, the present floor plan, and any proposed changes. Search out the right architect, contractor, and craftsmen to complete the restoration to your satisfaction. Inspect the house to uncover all the major and minor repairs necessary, find the salvageable material, and plan your construction sequence. Be sure to arrange your financing so that the cash flow insures necessary materials, salaries, and other expenses will be covered as the job progresses.

Photography: Steve Hogben

Above, several homes in Atlanta, Georgia's Inman Park can be seen, ranging from Queen Anne mansions to quaint Victorian cottages. Inman Park is a good example of a once elegant neighborhood falling inexorably into decline, then slowly given rebirth in dignity and popularity. Robert N. Griggs, a designer by profession, is the unanimously acclaimed founder and catalyst of the Inman Park revitalization.

The photo below illustrates the ever fascinating interplay of light and shadow across the decorative facade of a restored San Francisco home. Fish scale shingles, window fan, brackets, and trim add to the interest.

Photography: Val Hawes

A successful restoration job is made up of hundreds of decisions and details. The more of these items you have down on paper before construction starts, the smoother the restoration will be. Enough information to complete detailed preplanning is the secret.

2. **Be aware of the neighborhood.** No house is restored in a vacuum. Don't isolate your thinking and planning. Consider the setting for your home—the adjacent structures, the home facing yours, the entire block, and the property behind you. Rely on your previous neighborhood research to make changes and improvements in your house that are compatible with the area.

If yours is one of the first restoration projects in the neighborhood, you have taken on the added responsibility to provide a good example to encourage your neighbors to follow your lead. Retain the distinctive features of your home—maintain the size, scale, colors, and materials that are part of the neighborhood's established characteristics. This includes the landscaping, walkways, fencing, and gardens. Avoid introducing jarring elements into the neighborhood that destroy the relationship of your house to the surrounding territory.

Your decisions, particularly those which affect the exterior of your house, should be based on the knowledge of past appearances of your property. The restoration work can lead the revival in your neighborhood but don't get too far ahead of the crowd.

3. **Seek professional help.** Restoration is the most complex of construction projects de-

manding a wide range of talents and disciplines. No one individual has enough knowledge or time to cover each portion of the job and handle it successfully. Honestly weigh your skills, evaluate where your time can be most profitably spent, and retain professional assistance to handle the other areas. You may be a competent handyman but do you really know the details of the local building codes or the art of scheduling a work crew? Perhaps you are a long-time history buff but does this qualify you as a period architect? The research necessary for a restoration project is detailed and time-consuming. Could a professional do a more thorough job in a shorter time?

Any professional has built up an army of contacts over the years, and coupled with his experience, can usually save you both time and money. You substantially reduce your margin of error when you take advantage of professional expertise.

4. **Don't rush the job**. Take the necessary time to make sound decisions. Provide yourself with a cushion of time to solve unexpected problems or to take advantage of newfound information. Too often, important historical evidence is destroyed by an eager carpenter, lost through sanding or scraping, or thrown away during the cleanup process. Plan for periodic inspections as the job progresses so this material is not overlooked. You only have one chance to make these important discoveries.

Schedule your work at a steady pace. Allow for bad weather interruptions, late deliveries of materials, and unscheduled sickness of key workers. Some portions of the job must be done in strict sequence—wiring completed, building inspector okay's work, then wallcoverings are applied. At other times, when unforeseen delays occur, you can usually reschedule minor projects out of sequence. There is always plenty of detail work on any restoration project so temporarily missing materials or craftsmen should present no real emergency.

Plan the work in a logical sequence, allow for the unexpected and don't rush.

5. **Natural is not always normal**. For some reason, there is an overwhelming urge to strip everything away down to the natural material. Scrape the paint off the siding and the brickwork. Peel the wallpaper off down to the rough plaster. Tear down that plaster ceiling and expose those hand-hewn beams.

Don't let your enthusiasm carry you away. Rely on your historical research to be your guide. Yes, a Quaker farmhouse showcases the stark beauty of the unadorned natural materials. But if you are not restoring a

Quaker setting, stop before you go too far.

Our ancestors weren't that different from the homeowner of today. On the exterior, colorful paints added both decoration and a preservative coating to protect wood siding and brick from the weather. Victorians, in their lavish use of bright, multicolored exteriors, were downright gaudy when applying the paint brush.

On the interior, inexpensive pine was often carefully woodgrained to resemble more expensive oak or rosewood patterns and ornate, multicolored stencils were applied to walls and furniture as well as floors for a decorative effect. Brightly painted walls or heavily patterned wallpaper was the rule rather than the exception in most homes.

Interior restoration design can take its lead from the original millwork. In the top photo, fluting in the columns, between the living and dining rooms, is echoed in the fireplace mantel and surround. Below, a more simple and stately atmosphere is created by the geometric cleanliness of the raised wall mouldings. An interesting contrast between comfortable clutter and a feeling of quiet, almost austere, total control.

Photography: Bill Rooney

Photography: Wood Moulding and Millwork Producers

At times during a restoration project, there is a tendency to overrestore. However, not every portion of a home needs to be reworked. The stairway in the 1908 house in Granville, Ohio, shown above, would lose much of its charm and authenticity if the generation-worn treads were replaced with new material, and the unique hand painted risers were stripped or clumsily retouched. A little honest wear should be part of any authentic restoration project.

Only the earliest and most primitive houses had exposed wooden ceiling beams. Exposed beams were not considered attractive. Generally by the early 18th century, most ceilings were covered with plaster, often in ornate sculptured patterns reflecting the Greek, Roman, and Gothic geometry. Often the ceilings were paneled with detailed moulding applications.

Natural was not always normal. Be sure of your history before you go too far with your restoration.

6. **Don't overrestore or mix periods.** Another tendency to avoid is overrestoring—making the restoration look too new. Allow a little age to show through. Replacing material just because it shows signs of age is self-defeating. Stairtreads that have suffered the feet of generations should look worn. As long as the step is structurally sound and presents no safety hazard, let the wear show.

Replacing original bumpy plaster with a smooth new coat or scrubbing the smoke stains from a brick fireplace face destroy the patina of honest age.

Another method of overrestoring is

sometimes referred to as "earlying it up" or attempting to create an older building than originally existed. It is sort of like antiquing an entire house by artificially adding wear and tear, using material and styles that pre-date the actual house thus creating a false, unauthentic image.

Sometimes this "back-dating" is done through ignorance, and the only way to avoid this trap is to obtain sufficient research data in the beginning, and then follow through with an accurate restoration that reflects the true age, style, and period of the original structure. Occasionally, the over-restoring treatment is applied on purpose but professional historians frown on creating instant antiques and consider it a form of cheating. In most cases, the artificial attempt at aging a house is quickly detected by the trained eye. It seldom works and is totally unnecessary. If the structure is worth restoring, it is worth doing properly.

The only sin worse than overrestoring is mixing elements from different architectural periods. A colonial house with Victorian exterior trim surrounded by a Carpenter Gothic picket fence. Replacing windows, doors, and mantels around a fireplace requires a thorough knowledge of architectural styles. Your best defense against mixing parts from differing periods is a thorough understanding of the exact age and style of the house. Follow your research and avoid this restoration trap.

7. **Repair rather than replace.** Don't give up too quickly on badly deteriorated or damaged parts. Through haste or ignorance, too many old features that could be saved are consigned to the junk pile. With the modern materials and repair techniques available today, it is possible to salvage items that 20 years ago would have to be replaced.

Crumbling plaster can be strengthened. Masonry and brickwork can be rebuilt in place with the newer mortars. Steel beams or metal rods and mending plates can be used to shore up and reinforce weakened timbers. Patching compounds and waterproof glues can make amazing wood repairs.

The most revolutionary methods of preserving and strengthening rotted wood sections make use of the epoxy, polyester, and other modern synthetic resins. Badly deteriorated wood members are impregnated with these miracle materials, which harden in place and bond the weak wood fibers into a solid structural unit.

Whenever possible, attempt to make repairs before resorting to replacement parts.

8. **Avoid harsh methods.** Newer restoration techniques may be quick and easy but some are unnecessarily severe on old mate-

rials. Probably more damage has been done by sandblasting weathered brick than any other process. While the sandblasting removes old paint, it also destroys the hard, protective face skin of the brick exposing the softer and weaker interior material. Cleaning mortar joints with high-pressure water hoses or circular saw carbide blades usually does more damage than the treatment is worth.

In restoring brickwork, hand scraping and cleaning of the joints may be slower but it is considerably safer. Hand raking the joints and wire brushing the brick face is a gentler approach. Caution should be used when repainting mortar joints. The more modern portland cement mortar is considerably stronger than the old lime mortar. In brickwork, the basic rule is that the mortar should always be weaker than the stone or brick.

The use of steam and harsh chemicals can be dangerous. Cleaning brick or stripping wallpaper with steam equipment may freshen the surface but the introduction of excessive moisture into brick and plaster walls may create serious damage. Moisture in wood, masonry, or plaster should be avoided at all costs. Chemicals used to remove paint, wood finishes, and wallpaper should be applied with caution. Do not destroy the patina of age too quickly. Be careful that these harsh compounds don't splash on the surrounding areas and damage surfaces. Be sure to protect yourself with gloves and facemask from chemical splatter. Drop cloths will preserve the finish on nearby furniture and flooring.

Most restoration jobs are overscraped.

Paint stripping should be undertaken as a last resort. Most surfaces can be repaired and refinished without the mess and bother of stripping everything down to bare wood and plaster. Old wallpaper should be preserved wherever possible. Unless the paper is badly damaged, it is usually wise to attempt repairs, regluing, and minor touch-up. Methods are available to clean old paper surfaces without destroying the traditional patterns. Original wallpapers, particularly those dating back into the 18th century, are historically important and deserve preservation.

If you feel you must remove original paint, wallpaper, and wood finishes, salvage some of the material for analysis. These samples can be of big assistance in reproducing the look of original colors and patterns.

9. **Make mechanical repairs as inconspicuous as possible.** Heating ducts, plumbing pipes, and electrical wiring should be run in wall and floor cavities rather than surface-mounted. Consider having exterior electrical cables and telephone lines installed underground instead of strung to the side of the house. These unnecessary wires destroy the architectural lines of the structure.

Television antennas, roof vents, and air-conditioning units should be located as inconspicuously as possible. With a little planning, rooftop equipment can be hidden on the rear of the house, and clever landscaping with shrubs or trees will help mask these technical items.

Be sure that all mechanical work is completed in conformance with local safety, building, and fire codes.

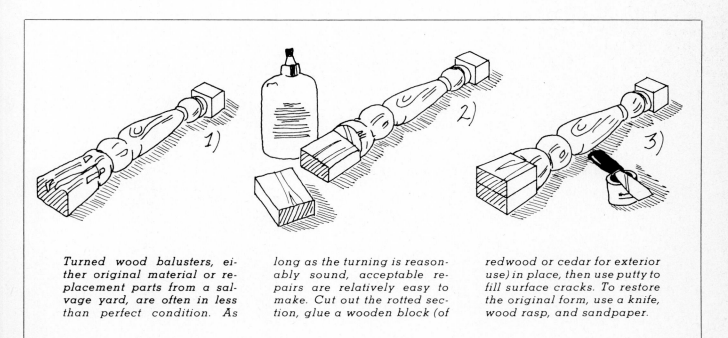

Turned wood balusters, either original material or replacement parts from a salvage yard, are often in less than perfect condition. As *long as the turning is reasonably sound, acceptable repairs are relatively easy to make. Cut out the rotted section, glue a wooden block (of* *redwood or cedar for exterior use) in place, then use putty to fill surface cracks. To restore the original form, use a knife, wood rasp, and sandpaper.*

Chapter 5
Nostalgia in the Present Tense

Restoration provides the opportunity to create an exciting, three-dimensional world. Traditional architects understood the interplay of light and shadow on finely carved woodwork, the depth and richness of brick, plaster, hardwoods and fabrics. This sensual approach to decorating is a major factor that separates the photos found in this chapter from the somewhat bland and two-dimensional homes of more recent vintage. There is a bold lustiness built into many restoration projects, where the owners were not afraid to accent ornate surfaces and highlight architectural elements with a splash of contrasting color, or play a rich wood grain against a neighboring painted or fabriced surface. These contrasts heighten individual elements, and when done with a feeling of historical accuracy, transform an exterior or an interior into a bold and lively statement—a personal expression of the individual tastes of those who live within the walls. Good restoration is not for the faint of heart.

The regal Queen Anne Victorian home, shown at the left, was built in 1890 by an affluent Atlanta businessman for his Philadelphia bride. Over the years, the once fashionable neighborhood had fallen on hard times and the mansion had been converted into eight substandard apartments. Fortunately, designer Robert Griggs and landscape architect Robert Aiken discovered the home, recognized its true potential and have restored it to its original splendor. At dusk, interior lights accent the turrets, the inviting wide veranda, and the fine, intricate millwork and quaint window collection.

The magnificent entry hall, shown below, establishes the tone for the entire home. The eye is drawn to the ornate marble-topped fireplace mantel, then up the sweeping staircase to the paneled and beamed ceiling. The natural hardwood floor and stairs blend with the woodwork, while the plants and fabric in the chair, rug, and window seat soften what might be an overpowering interior.

Photography: Steve Hogben

Photography: Chazz Sutphen

At the left, below, a San Francisco Victorian duplex apartment has been restored to a single family home. Twin entryways feature a pair of narrow doors which open for full access. The family wisely selected a dark color for the lap siding to set off the ornate exterior millwork. The hand-stenciled decorations on the three bay windows below and the pair of double windows on the upper story unify the busy facade.

Below, right, a trio of stately dowagers emphasizes the effect of restoration activity on an older neighborhood. These narrow, four-story Victorians offer a study in period window designs. The upper level of the center house illustrates unique 45-degree windows set in the corners, one of which opens onto a small balcony. For those energetic families willing to navigate the multi-level stairs, this set of city homes, perched on a hillside, offers an irresistible restoration challenge that can't be ignored.

The bedroom above, part of an 1840's house still under restoration, draws its charm from the simple, almost stark, interior treatment. One section of the steeply pitched roof intrudes into a corner of the small room, and the slanted ceiling line is echoed in the unusual double-triangle upper windows. A select few pieces of massive dark furniture contrast with the plain white walls, ceiling, and bed and window fabrics.

The exterior of the Robert Garrison House, shown to the right, is a classic example of Gothic Revival architecture. Projecting gables, the general asymmetry, the six-over-six pane first floor windows, and the front doorway's transom and sidelights confirm the styling. The simple three-color exterior paint scheme is more than adequate to highlight the millwork details. A fine example of a modest but surprisingly impressive house which gained greatly by a sensitive but sure restoration touch.

Photography: Val Hawes

Built in 1895 for winemaker Giacomo Migliavacca, the beautiful Victorian home shown to the left and below is now listed in the National Register of Historical Places. Constructed of the finest materials of the time, the upper stories are finished with imported Italian slate shingles. Turned wood porch railings are designed in a wagon wheel pattern, applied wooden scroll designs are found on each of the three roof gables and between window turrets, and most of the interior is done in oak. The original first floor consisted of a front parlor, sitting room, and reception hall complete with "coachman's corner," the second floor had five bedrooms and full Victorian bath, and the upper floor was used as a ballroom.

At right, a typical slanted-bay Italianate row house, probably built between 1875 and 1895, was given a bright elegant look by using a variety of colors (light blue, dark blue, white and sunny yellow) to highlight the facade, window and roof details. Normally, homes like this were stripped and stuccoed in later years, completely covering and destroying the intricate charm of their elaborate exteriors.

Below right, a fine example of Victorian Italianate styling, this imposing mansion was constructed in 1886 for Samuel E. Holden, president of Sawyer Tanning and Woolen Mills. It originally had eleven rooms including a library, music room, dining room, and parlor. The house features hand-carved oak woodwork, four fireplaces, 14-foot ceilings, stained glass windows, and solid redwood construction throughout. The present owners are Linda and Gerald Wuichet.

Photography: Ken Hilmer

The 1876 home at the left is large and sprawling in the late Victorian manner. However, the sparing application of exterior decoration may have been an economy measure on the part of the builder. The second story tower and high pitch of the gable focus attention on the original slate roof.

Below left, the warm and inviting sitting room is accented by a cast-iron fireplace with handsome maple clock on the mantel. Flocked wallpaper, braided rug, and needlepoint chairs add to the period look.

Below, right, an oversize corner cupboard of native hardwoods provides the perfect setting to display the homeowner's collection of mid and late 19th century glassware. Child's cane high chair and bentwood lamp stand are examples of period antiques found throughout the home.

The formal living room, shown to the right, contrasts sharply with the more inviting decor of the family room. Here, a more stately atmosphere is achieved with the carefully balanced oval picture frames flanking the tall clock. The cut glass ceiling chandelier reflects on the white marble mantel, casting a soft glow from the brass pails.

Photography: Chazz Sutphen

Photography: Chazz Sutphe

Far left, a perfect example of a small town Ohio home. Built, circa 1860, the house displays earlier, classical influences in the doorway and window treatments yet shows a more "modern" Victorian effect in the outer trim and arched front porch decorations. The home was purchased in 1964 and slowly restored by the owner with a sure and steady hand from its former dilapidated condition into its present picture postcard beauty.

The formal dining room, shown in the upper photo, is a rich combination of textures, wood grains and carefully selected colors. The deep blue fireplace front contrasts with the white cast iron grate in the hearth opening. Cane-back upholstered armchairs around the sparkling crystal on the table, and the tall bookcases along the wall add to the refined feeling.

The bedroom in the lower photo is dominated by a handsome turned tiger maple bedstead set off by the tester canopy.

A compact Victorian, shown in the upper left photo, still packs a lot of charm into three narrow stories. The wrought iron railing, atop the brick wall at street level, leads to a basement entrance door beneath the bay window. The unusual dividers between the bay window sections feature columns with fluted bottom sections. The band of latticework across the lower front facade cleverly hides an entrance door to the rear yard and garden.

The upper right hand photo illustrates single family and duplex homes in the traditional San Francisco Victorian styling. The similarity in decorative millwork indicates they were built at approximately the same time and, most likely, by the same carpenter. Square butt cedar shingles, applied in an offset pattern, accent the textured siding. The upper portion of the double-hung window sash employs small panes in the top sections. Eagles perched atop the porch dormers keep a watchful eye on the street.

A western farmhouse kitchen, at far left, has the table set for a hearty breakfast. Although not part of the original house, the kitchen wood burning stove, circa 1880, fits admirably with the period furnishings. High-backed wood chairs, checkered wallcovering and brick-like floor tile complete the cozy picture.

The exterior photo, above, shows the restored Albany, Oregon, farmhouse built in 1888 beside a branch of the Santiam Canal. When purchased in 1972, the owners stripped off the composition siding to reveal the original 8-inch drop wood siding. A new foundation was poured around the original brick piers; new gutters, roof and central heating were installed to make the home compatible with the Northwest climate.

The living room, below left, of the simple Italianate farmhouse was once two parlors. A remodeling project in 1927 removed the dividing wall, opening up the space into one large room. At the same time, the fireplace and hardwood floors were added. Today, the pair of upholstered chairs before the fireplace and the reading lamp with turned post supporting a fringed lampshade create an inviting picture. The enlarged room allows for a second seating arrangement in front of the prototype picture window.

The back door, shown below right, leads from the kitchen to the garden. Thanks to high ceilings, it was possible to install several shelves above the door in order to display a collection of antique gray graniteware cooking utensils.

Photography: Steve Marley

The marvelous Queen Anne home, shown below, is a classic example of persistance paying off if you are serious about playing the restoration game. The present owners had patiently waited as an elderly lady had allowed the house to fall into disrepair. During one of their regular "inspection" tours, they were crestfallen to discover a young couple had just bought their prize and were busy attempting to restore the home. However, eleven months later a real estate agent let them know the house was again available, and they snapped it up. It took a hectic eight months to complete the restoration. All the walls and ceilings were stripped, old wiring and plumbing replaced, baseboard heaters, a new roof and attic insulation were added. Today, the huge six bedroom home is completed and is the showplace of the neighborhood. One of the most enjoyable features of the home, built in 1895, is the spacious veranda circling the house. It makes an ideal spot for quiet reading even when it rains, as it has been known to do in damp Albany, Oregon.

The living room, shown at right, was enlarged during the restoration and the corner fireplace expanded. The upper surface was breasted with an ornate mantel, once a buffet. Large, paneled, pocket doors slide into the walls. All millwork was carefully stripped and refinished to capture the craftsmanship of an earlier age. The warm color scheme was selected to accent rich wood grains.

The before and after pictures on the right display the magic that can be worked during a well planned restoration project. An Early Victorian had been "modernized" with horrendous results. The sterilized exterior had lost any hint of personality. With the assistance of San Francisco Victoriana, research uncovered original documents detailing the lost millwork patterns. New siding, reapplication of decorative trim and a fresh coat of paint transformed an ordinary house into a charming home. The major improvement was restoring the stair railings, porch overhang and the small balcony beneath the second story front window.

Photography: Steve Marley

Photography: From the archives of
San Francisco Victoriana

Photography: Steve Marley

Photography: Val R. Hawes

Built by John C. Mitchell, an insurance broker, this Italianate-styled Victorian, shown at left, has proudly stood in the city of San Francisco for over 100 years. It survived the 1906 earthquake and fire, a neighborhood fire in 1913, and years of neglect and decay. Its present owner, attorney Philip Strauss, has given five years of time, money and persevering labor to its restoration. As one climbs the stairs to the home, the intricacies of the beautiful stained glass doors capture your imagination, and you're suddenly transported to an age gone by. Charming plaster garlands drape the interior walls, a gas-lit lamp atop the carved newel post flickers, and the exquisite parlor chandeliers captivate your attention with their sparkle. The fanciful fresco and imitation marble ceiling found in the dining room were painted by artist Eric Feighner in the Victorian tradition of simulating one material for another. Ceiling is actually composed of a heavy patterned wallpaper, lincrusta, divided by mouldings.

A most impressive room is the stenciled upstairs bedroom with adjoining bath. The stenciling design adorning the walls and executed by Feighner comes directly from a period stenciling book. The adjoining bath has plaster walls painted to simulate marble and contains a sink and tub only, as was Victorian custom. The toilet is housed in a separate closet-like room around the corner.

The Queen Anne style home was first designed in England by Richard Norman Shaw, and was introduced in the United States by architect Henry Hobson Richardson in the early 1870s. The home shown, above right, is an example of the Queen Anne style as found in San Francisco. Shingle-covered gable roof, multi-stories, turret, bay window, many small details, and a variety of surface textures as seen in this home are inherent to the design. Painted a baby blue, with details in a soft cream, the home bespeaks a bygone era and a time of luxury.

Some 48,000 Victorian houses were built in San Francisco between the gold rush and 1915. Many were lost in the 1906 earthquake, but many still remain. Unfortunately, a vast number of these homes were stripped of their ornamentation, covering up their Victorian charm with stucco, aluminum siding, and various other materials. One type of Victorian restoration project involves installing some replacement millwork and a fresh paint job using carefully coordinated colors. Depending on the house's condition, an average two-story home can be repainted for $3,000. The photo at upper left illustrates the great revival movement, a multi-story Victorian returned to its illustrious presence.

Photography: From the archives
of San Francisco Victoriana

The before and after photos shown on these two pages perfectly illustrate the architectural crimes committed in the name of progress. Well-meaning homeowners of earlier generations "improved" these fine old structures by stripping away their individuality and reducing them to bland, ordinary faces. San Francisco Victoriana, formed by a group of dedicated craftsmen-historians to fight this architectural blight, have succeeded in reclaiming the former beauty of these three urban homes.

At the far left, the original structure lost all detailing under a uniform coat of paint. The modest restoration effort capitalized on the rich decorative elements by setting each apart through a carefully coordinated color scheme. The obvious humanizing effect of plants and shrubbery is evident in this elegant but simple restoration.

The pair of before and after photos on this page follows the same basic improvement plan—research, restore and accent the individual elements. The single family house, above left, accented the horizontal lines by replacing sections of the plain stucco surface with lap siding, a dark colored band between the second and third stories, and contrasting light colors on the porch railings. Additional handpainted decorations at the eaveline reinforced the horizontal feeling.

The Victorian duplex reversed the procedure by accenting the vertical thrust of the twin bay window units and entryway. The original horizontal siding was masked by a contrasting color plan which added visual height to the structure. Treatment of the roofline by installing and highlighting the vertical decorative millwork contributed further to the elongation process. These dramatic changes emphasize the importance of professional assistance in restoration.

Chapter 6
Exterior Restoration

xterior restoration should follow the general step-by-step sequence outlined earlier. Make the house weathertight, correct major foundation and structural problems, then attack the repair and replacement phase before completing the final finish work, landscaping, adding walks and paths, gardens and fencing. In this chapter and the succeeding ones, detailed information on materials and methods is included for several reasons. Either you will be personally involved in doing much of the individual work yourself or you will be supervising a contractor and his crew doing the actual restoration. In either case, it is important that you fully understand how the work should be performed and that it be done in a competent and safe manner to meet all building codes and retain the historic flavor of your house.

Restoring a home can seem like an overwhelming task at first, but with sufficient preplanning, careful inspection, and a willingness to learn as you go, the job can be completed by anyone with normal handyman skills. Now is the time to start collecting specific information. Investigate the library and newsstands for books and periodicals with repair information. Contact the various product manufacturers for details on sizes, colors, and grades of materials. Most companies supply carefully illustrated application or installation booklets that can be very helpful. Break your restoration project down into manageable components and file your information by specific project areas.

Roof Repairs

A weathertight house usually starts with a sound roof. While your initial house inspection may have indicated some water damage, you will now need to conduct a careful investigation to determine the exact location of the problem spots and how they can best be cured. Start in the attic with a flashlight. Look for water stains and discolor-

Photography: From the archives of San Francisco Victoriana

Photography: Leo Pinard

Opposite page, scaffolding provides the safest and most efficient method to handle exterior repairs. Commercial scaffolding can be rented at nominal cost. Above, a weather-tight roof is usually the first major task completed before any detail or interior decorative work can be started.

ation along the rafters, on the roofboards or the attic floor. Pay particular attention to areas around the chimney, soil stack or vent sleeves, at the ridge, hip and valley locations on the roof. Water runs down hill, so you will have to trace back from floor stains or rafter discoloration upward until you can determine just where the water is entering the attic. Turn off the flashlight and look upward to spot any daylight leaking through the roof. Record those areas you know you can locate from the rooftop, i.e., around the chimney or vent stacks. Leaks on the open roof area are tougher to locate from the outside. Here, drill a small hole through the roof from within the attic and work a small length of wire through the hole until it protrudes through the roof. Now you can spot the problem area from the top side of the roof.

Over the years, sun, wind, ice, and snow, as well as extreme temperature changes, take their toll on any roof. When inspecting the surface, look for obvious problems. Strong

When inspecting your roof, look for cupped, split or missing shingles.

Chimneys and vent pipes may need caulking or new flashing.

Torn hip or ridge shingles, exposed to high winds, must be replaced.

Winds can pop roofing nails so they no longer contact shingles.

Bare spots indicate granules have worn away from shingle surface.

Granules collecting in gutters and downspouts mean excessive wear.

Photography: Celotex Corp.

winds may have loosened the shingles and popped the nails. Wood shingles may be badly split, curled, or rotted. Nails may have rusted out. A falling tree limb may have smashed roof tile or slate shingles.

Avoid walking directly on the ridge, hip, or valley areas. Step over or around rather than on these elements to avoid further damage. Check the flashing and caulking around the chimneys, vents, skylights, and TV antennas. Inspect the general roof surface for damaged or missing shingles and bare spots, where age and weather have thinned out asphalt shingle surface granules. Finally, look at the gutters, gutter hangers, and downspouts. If gutters are clogged with leaves and debris, water will be forced back up under the shingles to soak the eaves and dampen interior walls.

Minor roof repairs are fairly simple to make. Loose shingles and nails can be renailed. Flashing is simple to recaulk and seal, gutters are easily cleaned and relined. However, extensive damage usually calls for a complete reroofing.

Before starting a roof inspection or repair work, consider the potential danger involved. If heights make you uncomfortable, leave this portion of the restoration project to others. There is plenty of work in other areas where you can display your talents. If heights don't make you break out in a cold sweat, keep the following safety suggestions in mind. A wet roof is always hazardous—stay off until the footing is dry. Wear sneakers or rubber-soled boots for secure footing. Ladder work can be tricky unless you are familiar with safety procedures. Always provide enough lean to the ladder so your weight moves into the building side as you climb. Make sure the ladder base is on firm, even footing. Use blocks or wedges to level the base area. For safety, the ladder top should extend several feet above the roofline. This provides a safe handhold at that critical point on the roof edge when climbing or descending. Bundles of wood shakes or asphalt shingles are awkward and heavy (often more than 100 pounds) to carry up a ladder. Break the bundles apart and carry up partial loads.

When working on steeply pitched roof sections, it may be necessary to nail lumber footing cleats to the surface for safe traction. Drive nails through the wood and roof into the rafters below. Any nail holes can be plugged later with roofing cement. It is sometimes possible to tie a ladder to steep surfaces, securing one end to the ridge or tying the top to a chimney. A tool belt with nail pouch will keep hammer or shingle hatchet, knife, measuring tape, and nails handy. For safe footing, keep material on the roof to a minimum.

Reroofing with slate or tile is usually a job for the professionals. Special tools and skills are needed with these materials and unless you have done the job before, you are probably wiser to let an experienced roofer do the repair work. However, replacing a wood or asphalt shingle roof can be done with ordinary hand tools and minimal skills. It is not a particularly easy job, tough and tedious is a good description, but by following directions and taking your time to do the detailed trim work, you can handle the project by yourself.

Wood and asphalt shingles are sold by the square. A square equals the amount of material needed to cover 100 square feet, a 10-foot by 10-foot area. By using a little trigonometry, it is possible to estimate the amount of material needed from the ground. But it is usually quicker and more accurate to take your dimensions directly from the roof surface. Multiply the length of the roof by the width on major sections to get the square footage. Individual, odd-shaped sections should be estimated as closely as possible. For instance, a dormer roof section may be triangular in shape but it will have a duplicate but reversed triangular shape on the other side. Measure the right angle ridge and rake dimensions and figure the footage as if the section were square in shape (a square cut in half diagonally).

Total up the square footage for all roof surfaces and divide by 100 to give you the number of roofing squares needed for the job. Now, since the ridges, hip, and valley sections require extra material for trimming, measure the total length of these areas and add one extra square for every 100 feet of length. This will be your grand estimated total for buying your roofing by the square.

The next step is to decide whether or not you must remove the old roofing before applying the new material. Some professional roofers insist that the old roof must come off. Others recognize that overroofing can provide a double roof with extra insulation value and storm protection. Your decision should be based on the following questions:

1. Are the roof boards in good shape or are they rotted, badly split, or warped? Obviously, no roofing job is any better than the surface to which it is applied. If the roof boards are not in sound condition, the roofing must be removed to replace the boards.

2. Is the present roofing in good condition? Is the surface reasonably flat, shingles in good shape and free of moss in the shaded portions of the roof?

3. Are you able to locate and nail into solid wood boards or strips under the present roofing? You must be able to tie a new roof into solid backing.

4. How many roof layers are already in place? Many building codes limit the total number of roofs on a structure to no more than three. Each succeeding layer adds hun-

dreds of pounds of weight to the rafters and you are not permitted to overload the structure for obvious reasons.

In reroofing, particularly with asphalt shingles, you must realize that the new top layer probably will not lie perfectly smoothly. Any bumps or ridges in the original roof will be magnified by the new covering. Usually this is not a critical difference, but you should be aware of this factor when making your decision.

Wood Shingles

When overroofing with wood shingles, it is necessary to properly prepare the roof surface. A six-inch-wide strip of existing shingles must be removed from all eaves and gable ends. New 1x6-inch boards are nailed down in the stripped back areas. Then the original ridge and hip coverings must be taken off and replaced with a strip of redwood or cedar beveled siding on either side with the thick butt edges overlapping at the peak. Sweep down the roof to remove any dirt or debris, and you are ready to start.

Be sure to use nails long enough to penetrate into the roof sheathing under the old roof. Either 5 penny, 1¾-inch or 6 penny, 2-inch-long nails will usually do the job. Be sure they are rust-resistant aluminum or hot-dipped galvanized nails. You'll need approximately 2 pounds per square. Try to use nails and flashing materials of the same metal. Don't mix aluminum nails with galvanized flashing or the reverse. When exposed to moisture, dissimilar metals will cause a chemical corrosive reaction.

Wood shingles and handsplit shakes are available in several lengths and grades. To

If your existing roof is in sound condition, it may be possible to apply a new roof over the old. Below, 18-inch wide asphalt felt is applied, then a started course of shingles, which extends one inch beyond the roof edge.

Photography: Red Cedar Shingle & Handsplit Shake Bureau

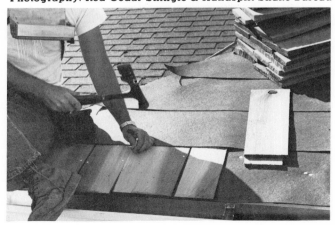

determine the shingle exposure, refer to the manufacturer's instructions for your particular roof pitch. Or contact the Red Cedar Shingle & Handsplit Shake Bureau in Bellevue, Washington, for their detailed installation brochure, which also illustrates the proper methods for handling flashing, ridge, hip, and valley construction.

Start your roofing job with a double thickness of shingles at the bottom edge of the roof. Make sure that the shingles overlap several inches beyond the eave edge so that rain water will run off and drip into the center of your gutters. A shingler's hatchet with a corrugated nailing head, adjustable exposure guide, and sharp blade is an invaluable tool for the job.

Use two nails per shingle no matter what the width. Place the nails about 3/4 inch from the shingle side and drive the nails down until the heads just meet the shingle surface. Any deeper and you risk splitting the wood. Don't butt shingles tightly side by side; leave at least 1/4-inch gap to allow shingles to expand and prevent warping when wet. Shingles must be spaced with joints at least 1½ inches apart from joints in the course below. This prevents water from running down one joint to the joint directly below.

Asphalt Shingles

Asphalt shingles are available in a wide selection of colors, weights, patterns, and styles. Lighter weights, 235 pounds per square, are good for about 20 years, while heavier weights, 350-450 pounds per square, last 25 years or more. Shingles are available with several fire-resistant ratings, so check your local building codes to determine what is required in your area.

Depending on your present roof construction and the number of layers already in place, asphalt shingles may be used to over-roof either wood or asphalt shingles. The ideal temperature for laying asphalt shingles is approximately 70 degrees. In hotter weather, the shingles become soft and gummy, difficult to cut, and may become damaged by foot traffic. Colder weather, below 40 degrees, presents different problems. Shingles are stiff, brittle, and subject to cracking when handling and nailing.

Asphalt shingle overroofing preparation is similar to that used for wood shingles. Cut back old shingles and install 1x6 boards at the eaves and rake edges; remove ridge and hip coverings. Hot-dipped galvanized roofing nails that have large flat heads and are long enough to penetrate to the roof sheath-

Photography: Red Cedar Shingle & Handsplit Shake Bureau

The first course of shakes is applied over started course with 1/2-inch expansion spacing.

Anti-rust painted, 26-gauge metal valley is first nailed in place. New metal should not touch old metal.

Shakes are angle cut and applied over metal valley to provide 6-inch wide gutter.

Felt overlaps top 4-inch of shakes and long nails penetrate sheathing at least 1/2-inch.

Shakes are angle cut at hip line; shingler's hatchet speeds nailing and trimming.

The factory-assembled "hip-and-ridge" units are lapped to make weather-tight joints.

Photography: Asphalt Roofing Mfrs. Assn.

Asphalt shingles are available in a variety of colors, textures and patterns for any restoration need. Here, three-dimensional asphalt shingles are installed over an old, but sound, existing wood shingle roof.

ing are used. Begin shingling by applying starter strips recommended by the manufacturer to the eaves to thicken the roof's edge. Read directions that are supplied with the shingles carefully or write to the Asphalt Roofing Manufacturers Association in New York City. Their literature will supply the details on proper exposure for different types of shingles, and the procedures for handling ridges, valleys, and flashing around chimneys and vent stacks.

In hot weather, it is important that asphalt shingles be stored properly to avoid problems. Bundles should be stacked crisscross fashion, not more than three feet high and always in the shade to prevent the self-sealing adhesive from sticking.

Part of weatherproofing your house includes repair of the gutters and downspouts. If neglected, this water drainage system will cause problems at the roofline, walls, and foundation. If the original gutters are in reasonably good condition, you may need nothing more than an inspection to make sure they are clean and free-flowing. Check to make sure gutter hanger straps or spikes are nailed tightly. Do the same thing with straps holding the downspouts in place. They should keep the spout tight against the siding of the house.

Downspouts should have wire strainers or baskets installed in the gutter opening to prevent leaves from clogging the water flow. At the bottom, all downspouts should have a concrete splash block to channel rain water away from the foundation.

Partially rusted gutters and downspouts should be wire-brushed to remove loose rust, then primed and repainted. If metal gutters

have been rusted through in several spots, it is possible to patch the holes with fiberglass and epoxy resins. The same treatment can be used to repair damaged wooden gutters but then the entire gutter interior should have a preservative coat of tar-like material brushed on to retard further deterioration. Your local building material supplier can guide you in selecting the appropriate primer, paint, and patching compounds. But remember to select compatible metals when doing repair work. Don't apply aluminum gutters with galvanized nails. Use like metals in all cases.

Badly rusted or rotted gutters will have to be replaced. If the original gutters are in place, select replacements of the same size if they appear adequate to handle the water run-off. Roofs less than 750 square feet in size can use 4-inch gutters; those up to 1,400 square feet, a 5-inch size; larger areas will need a 6-inch gutter to drain properly.

When installing new gutters, remember you are constructing a water drainage system, so plan ahead to provide the needed slope and proper location for downspouts. Gutters must slope a minimum of 1/2 inch for every 20 feet of run. A 1-inch slope will help the water travel faster but may look out of horizontal when judged against the roofline or siding. A 3/4-inch slope is a good compromise. The general rule is that any gutter run that is less than 20 feet in length can drain into a single downspout at one end. Anything longer requires a high center that slopes to downspouts at each end.

Your exterior investigation should include a close inspection of gutters and downspouts. Badly rusted or damaged gutters will spill rain water down siding, or more often create serious problems when water backs up under eaves.

Photography: Bill Rooney

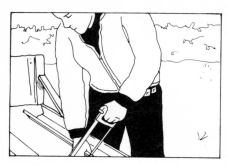

Measure carefully, then assemble on ground, cutting with hacksaw.

Gutter sections and end caps are riveted with a hand riveter.

After riveting, all joints must be sealed to make seams water-tight.

Outlet tube for downspout is located and riveted in place.

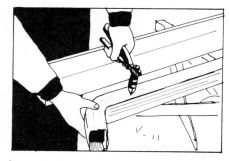

Bottom elbow is slipped over downspout and riveted before it is raised.

Fascia bracket hangers are placed on 30-inch centers.

Assembled, riveted and sealed, sections are raised into place.

Gutter section is snapped into place and secured with fascia hangers.

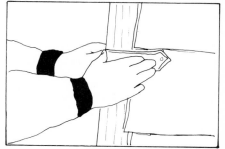

The downspout is attached to house side with bands and nails or screws.

Source: Kaiser Aluminum Corp.

Foundation Repairs

Since the foundation supports the entire house, it must be considered the most critical element in a restoration project. Unless the foundation is sound, solid, and level, the house frame may be distorted, windows and doors racked out of square, and siding or brickwork cracked and loosened. The problem is twofold—effective repairs must be made, and at the same time, those conditions that created the problem in the first place must be eliminated.

Foundation construction falls into several categories. Some houses may have masonry walls of stone or brick bonded with mortar. Others may be supported on masonry piers or posts. More recent houses may have concrete foundations, and in some sections of the country, wood pier post foundations were common. In almost all cases, no matter what type foundation, wood plate or sill timbers sat directly on the foundation and supported the wall and floor framing.

Minor foundation problems can usually be repaired. Deteriorating and crumbling mortar can be removed and brick and stone work repointed. Hairline cracks in concrete can be filled, and piers, if they are still structurally sound, can usually be jacked and wedged into a level position. Major foundation problems are another story.

Whether your foundation is masonry, concrete, or wood, excessive moisture is the most common villain. Not only does water damage the foundation, but, if allowed to continue, it eventually attacks the wood sill or plate resting on the foundation. Surface water is the most common source of dampness. Rain water from downspouts must be channeled away from the foundation with splash blocks. Proper grading around the house perimeter requires that landscaping slope away from the foundation. A high water table is a more serious situation, but foundation waterproofing and installation of footing drain tiles may minimize the problem.

If stone and brick foundations are in poor shape—crumbling mortar, cracked stones, or spalled brick from the expansion of frozen moisture—then the foundation usually must be rebuilt. In most cases, severely cracked or bowed concrete foundations get progressively worse and demand major repair efforts. Excessive dampness that has rotted wood foundations, piers and sills, or attracted insect damage, must be repaired or replaced. Serious foundation problems are pretty obvious. If you suspect you have trouble, you almost always have a more serious situation than is first evident.

Major foundation repair is *not* a job for the amateur. Professional skills and equipment are needed. In most cases, extensive excavation is required, then the entire house is often jacked up and propped in place while the repairs are made. If you have ever seen this done or watched a house being moved from one location to another site, you can appreciate the engineering skill needed to raise a house without destroying it.

It may be possible to excavate with a backhoe for major portions of the job, but some of the detail work will require hand pick and shovel labor. When the foundation has been exposed and repaired, take the opportunity to prevent the problems from recurring. Exterior foundation walls can be coated with waterproofing compounds to prevent water absorption. Drain tile should be installed at the foundation footings to collect and lead surface water away.

At the same time, you should inspect chimney and fireplace footings. These are usually separate from the house foundation and supported by their own footings. While the foundations are exposed, conduct a careful check for decay and insect damage of all wood parts. Decay thrives in moderate temperatures and moist conditions. Look for discolored wood and probe with a sharp knife to locate soft or spongy wood members. Sound wood will break off in long slivers or splinters while rotted sections are brittle and tend to break off in small chunks.

Rotted wood parts can sometimes be saved by using the newer epoxy resin compounds. Most are a two-part formula, which is mixed, loaded into a narrow-nosed applicator, and forced into the wood through 1/2-inch holes drilled into the damaged area. As the compound is forced into the holes, it spreads throughout the rotted section where

Photography: Peg Pinard

Major foundation repairs often require equipment and professional skills.

In high water table areas, a pump may be needed to remove water from hole.

Even with power equipment, hand shovel is used for detail work.

Once excavated, foundation position is carefully laid out for forms.

Lumber and plywood is used to create the hollow foundation concrete forms.

Wet concrete is heavy. Extensive form bracing is required before pour begins.

Wet concrete is pumped into forms, then vibrated for solid compaction.

New foundation is allowed to cure before house is lowered into place.

it dries and hardens. The epoxies are expensive but may be the only reasonable method of salvaging wood structural parts. The alternative is to jack up the house, remove the rotted and decayed sections, and replace them with new treated wood members. The U.S. Government Printing Office in Washington offers an excellent booklet, *Epoxies for Wood Repairs in Historic Buildings*, illustrating the materials and methods used.

Wood destroying insects are termites, powderpost beetles, and carpenter ants. Subterranean termites, those which have direct access to the ground, are most common. Their most obvious sign is earthen tunnels built over the foundation to provide passage tubes from the ground to the wood above. Nonsubterranean termites are found along the southern coastal states. Here, swarms of small-winged insects and small piles of fine sawdustlike leavings indicate their presence. Soil poisoning by a professional exterminator is necessary to eliminate them.

Powderpost beetles leave small deposits of fine wood flour behind. Damaged wood areas appear to have been blasted with birdshot, marking the wood with a pattern of fine holes. Sometimes the homeowner can eliminate the beetles with insecticides, but severe cases will require fumigation by a professional exterminator. Carpenter ants, as the name implies, chew right through wood. They don't eat the material but nest in the wood. They can be identified by piles of coarse sawdust outside their entrance holes. To destroy carpenter ants, an approved insecticide is blown into the hollow galleries killing the colony.

Foundation repair work requires a high degree of skill and technical knowledge. This is one area where professional assistance is required for successful restoration.

Siding Restoration

Siding materials range from brick and stone, to adobe in the Southwest, to wood shingles or beveled lap siding in a variety of patterns. But before starting any siding restoration work, you should assure yourself that the repairs can be done efficiently and safely. This means you will need scaffolding—a raised framework with plank platform for safe footing. Don't attempt to make major siding repairs from a ladder. You will spend more time running up and down, moving ladder positions, and juggling tools and materials with one hand while you hang on with the other.

You can construct your own one-story scaffolding with 2x4 lumber, cross-bracing, and lumber planks. Two-story scaffolding requires 2x6 material for the vertical supports with 2x4s for bracing. Use two-headed, duplex, or scaffolding nails for construction. These fasteners let you construct the framework solidly, yet the extra nail head makes it easy to disassemble and move the scaffold.

You can construct your own scaffolding, but it is often smarter and safer to rent commercial scaffolding. The cost is nominal, the metal framework sturdier and easier to assemble and disassemble, plus most scaffolding comes with adjustable screw jack legs, which save time when working on uneven ground. Be sure to rent sufficient scaffold planking at the same time. This lumber, usually 2x10 or 12 inches wide, is a special grade vertical grain wood that is considerably stronger than the normal flat grain boards available at the local lumberyard.

You can locate scaffolding rental operations under Scaffolding or Construction Rental Equipment in the local Yellow Pages. Most rental agreements are for a one-month period, which normally provides sufficient time to make repairs and do siding finish work. When possible, plan to work and complete one portion of the house before you move to the next section. This will reduce the amount of disassembly and reassembly of scaffolding sections.

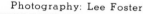

Wood destroying insects can be a sign of real trouble for any restoration project. Below, mud tunnel is created by termites to maintain direct earth-to-wood contact. Soil poisoning will exterminate them.

Photography: Lee Foster

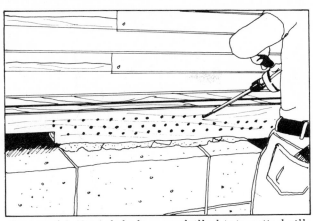

Series of 1/2-inch holes are drilled into rotted sill.

Special epoxy consolidant is squeezed into holes.

Chemical spreads into and hardens fibers as it dries.

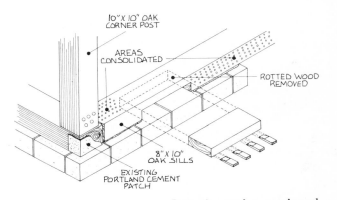

10" X 10" OAK
CORNER POST

AREAS
CONSOLIDATED

ROTTED WOOD
REMOVED

8" X 10"
OAK SILLS

EXISTING
PORTLAND CEMENT
PATCH

*Rotted wood is replaced
or chemically consolidated.*

Before getting the scaffolding, sketch out the job dimensions and plan for the amount of material needed. Scaffolding usually comes in 10-foot-wide sections. For a 30-foot-long house side you need two 10-foot tower sections set 10 feet apart with extra planks and guard rail to bridge the gap.

When erecting scaffolding, keep the following safety rules in mind.

1. Be extra careful when erecting steel scaffolding near overhead power lines.

2. On uneven ground, don't rely on wood blocking, use the adjustable screw jacks for safe footing.

3. The scaffolding must be plumb and level. All braces and guard rails must be fastened securely.

4. Planking should be secured with nails and should not extend an unsafe distance beyond supports.

5. Consult the rental agency for safe load limits. Never overload the scaffolding with excess workers or construction material.

6. Finally, make sure your scaffolding is high enough for the job. Using stepladders or makeshift devices on top of the scaffold can be dangerous.

Masonry Restoration

The term "masonry" refers to any construction using stone or brick material bonded together with mortar. The mortar is nothing more than the glue or nonstructural material that binds the structural stone or brick into a solid unit. The general rule is that the mortar should be weaker than the structural material so that it acts as a slight cushion to provide flexibility to the wall.

Masonry damage is most often caused by dampness, particularly the freezing and thawing action of trapped water, excessive traffic vibration, severe air pollution, or poor structural design and workmanship. Water damage may cause crumbling mortar or spalling and surface disintegration on stone or brick faces. Major structural cracks and bulges require specialized professional repair, but minor and spot defects can usually be adequately fixed by a homeowner.

Exposed wood around doorway and windows in a stucco house can allow water to enter and disintegrate wood. Water works its way down inside and rots the entire frame.

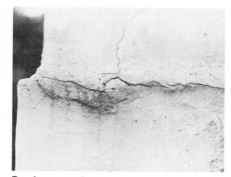

Professional inspectors often find more than they are looking for. Here, a termite inspector found a crack high on the outside chimney that allowed water to drain into timbers.

Cracks in the front step allow water to drain onto wood members below, rotting them. Damaged plaster must be removed, replaced, and caulked to assure a waterproof surface.

Photography: Lee Foster

A first-class restoration job requires that you take the extra step to match new materials to the existing siding. Replacement brick or stone may be easier to match than you suspect. Early masonry was not uniform in color, and you should try to match the tone range rather than an individual brick or stone. You may be able to find replacement material at local suppliers or salvage yards. Perhaps you can cannibalize masonry parts from inconspicuous areas of the house and use them to rebuild the more visable sections. One word of caution: Old bricks vary in quality, and it was common practice to use lower quality bricks in unexposed areas. Any exterior brickwork demands quality material. A brick is not a brick. If you are not able to distinguish first quality from lesser grades, better have an expert obtain your replacement materials.

The toughest part of masonry restoration is matching the color and physical properties of new mortar. The standard premixed bagged mortar is not acceptable for restoration work. Until the late nineteenth century, mortar was composed of lime, sand or clay, and water. It was relatively soft, provided flexibility to the wall, and depending upon the sand color, was of a pure white or tan-white tone. Modern portland cement is gray and extremely hard, which can lead to potential physical damage to softer stone or brick. White portland cement is closer in color to most original mortar but, in addition to being hard, it tends to shrink slightly as it sets, resulting in tiny cracks which may allow water absorption. Patented or masonry cement, combining portland cement with gypsum and limestone, is the safest mortar mix for accurate restoration. It is available in a number of premixed colors to match your needs.

Joint preparation can be a slow process, but one that cannot be rushed with mechanical aids. Under no circumstances should the joints be sawed with an abrasive blade. The saw blade will invariably cut into the brick or stone, damaging the corners and edges. Badly deteriorated mortar can be scraped from the point by hand with an old screwdriver or chisel. Crumbling mortar must be removed to a depth of 1 inch, then the joint is flushed with a hose to wash out dust and loose particles. When applying the new mortar, don't attempt to fill the gap with one big glob. The mortar should be applied in 1/4-inch layers and built up gradually. Keep the joints damp but not soaking wet as you work. The moisture prevents the stone or brick from absorbing the dampness from the mortar before it has time to set up properly.

When the final layer of mortar has been applied and allowed to harden slightly, it is raked with the appropriately shaped tool to match existing joints. A local masonry supply house can provide square, convex, or concave jointing tools. Once the mortar is dry, but before it hardens completely, scrape off any excess. Bristle brushes and plain water can be used to scrub off any mortar smeared on the brick face.

Entire masonry surfaces can be cleaned, but not everyone wants an older building to be as bright and clean as a new one. The decision is yours. Before attempting any surface cleaning, allow new mortar to cure for at least two weeks. A mild muriatic acid solution can be scrubbed onto a damp surface and then hosed off. Hard stone can be dry-sandblasted under pressure of 90 to 100 pounds of air. Brickwork and soft stone should never be sandblasted. High pressure water or steam cleaning can be effective methods, but are difficult for the amateur to handle, and care must be taken to avoid saturating the masonry surface with excessive amounts of moisture.

Stucco repairs require mineral pigments added to the final mortar coat to match existing surfaces. Minor cracks should be scraped open to sound stucco, then widened with a chisel on the inside surface. This produces a key crack, wider at the bottom than the top, which locks the new stucco into place. Large surface repairs usually require removing the damaged stucco down to the bare wall surface. Wire mesh or lath is nailed to the wall so that it extends at least 1/4 inch from the surface.

Stucco is usually applied in a three-coat process. The first, or scratch coat, is approximately 1/2-inch thick and should be pushed through the wire lath to assure a good bond. When the first coat is firm but not completely hard, it is scratched to form horizontal ridges. These supply a key or tooth for the second coat. The second or brown coat is applied about 3/8-inch thick and smoothed out slightly below the finished wall surface. This is moist cured for several days, then allowed to dry for a week. The final or top coat should be at least 1/8-inch thick and color-toned to match the surrounding stucco.

Stucco repairs, including color matching, moisture and application techniques, and curing times, differ slightly with temperature and climatic conditions. Consult a local supply house for recommendations covering your particular restoration situation.

Wood Siding Repair

Split and rotted sections of wood clapboard siding or wood shingles must be repaired before the damage spreads. It is necessary in order to prevent water from leaking into the walls and discourage insects from entering. Water will cause paint to peel from surrounding areas and hasten swelling and rotting of adjacent material.

Cracks in otherwise solid boards should be wedged open slightly with a chisel or large screwdriver along the length of the split. A waterproof exterior glue is forced into the opening with a thin knife blade and spread along the entire crack. The split is then closed by forcing the board together and nailing upward from the bottom to keep the crack closed. Use rustproof nails or screws for warped sections. Countersink the hardware slightly below the siding surface and fill the hole with putty for a smooth paintable surface.

When a clapboard is split in several places or badly rotted, it should be removed and replaced with sound material. You may be able to find matching parts from around your own house, from a salvage yard or local building material supply house. To remove a damaged section without destroying the surrounding siding, drive several wooden wedges beneath the rotted section to force it slightly away from the surface. This will provide a small opening so that a hacksaw blade can be slid up under the board to cut off nails that hold the section in place.

Special handles are sold for hacksaw blades, or simply wrap a used blade with tape at one end to provide a safe grip. Work the blade up and down until the nails are cut. Now, using a backsaw, make two vertical cuts, one at each end of the damaged section, until the piece can be removed.

Cut a replacement siding section to fit, and tap it up into place beneath the siding above, lining it up carefully with the adjacent siding sections. Nail it in place, countersink and putty the nail heads, and apply caulking compound to the seams at each end of the new piece. Apply a coat of exterior primer and finish with one or two coats of matching house paint.

Replacing wood shingles or shakes follows the same repair method. Use wood wedges to open a slight gap, insert a hacksaw blade to cut the nails above, then carefully split off the damaged area with a chisel. Be careful not to damage the shingles or building paper beneath. Insert new shingles and nail into place.

Fresh cedar or redwood clapboard and shingles will stand out like a sore thumb against weathered, grayed material. This color difference will fade in time as the new sections are exposed to the elements. However, you can hasten the matching process by applying several coats of ordinary household bleach to the new wood. Brush it on and the chemical bleaching action will develop a soft driftwood gray color. Commercial finishes are available to do the same job so you might get a recommendation from the neighborhood paint store if you have a substantial amount of new wood to treat.

Window and Door Repair

Windows, sometimes called "the eyes of the house," are often taken for granted in a restoration project. Sloppy repairs, arbitrary replacement of different sizes and styles of sash, or mixing of glass types, can destroy exterior authenticity. Pay attention to your historical research and take extra pains to reproduce the look and feel of old windows.

Window sash is an overlooked part of the early cabinetmaker's art. The typical 18th-century sash featured a dozen small 6x8-inch glass panes, and the standard twelve-over-twelve window required 22 mortise and tendon joints per sash. Unless you are an

Parts of a double-hung window

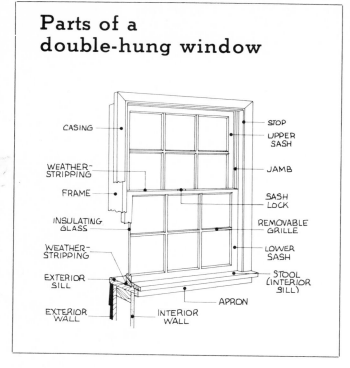

- CASING
- WEATHER-STRIPPING
- FRAME
- INSULATING GLASS
- WEATHER-STRIPPING
- EXTERIOR SILL
- EXTERIOR WALL
- STOP
- UPPER SASH
- JAMB
- SASH LOCK
- REMOVABLE GRILLE
- LOWER SASH
- STOOL (INTERIOR SILL)
- APRON
- INTERIOR WALL

experienced woodworker with a shaper and selection of moulding cutterhead knives, you should not attempt to recreate antique window parts. Several professional craftsmen are now reproducing these old millwork items, or you may be able to find replacements at a local glass dealer, salvage company, antique dealer, or farm auction.

Old glass was originally imported from England for colonial homes but after 1792, when the Boston Crown Glass Company began production, most glass was domestically manufactured. Early glassmaking used the crown method where a large sphere of molten glass was attached to a pontil iron or punty rod, heated and spun until centrifugal force produced a large flat disc. This was cut into glass sizes, and the center portion where the rod was attached produced the characteristic bull's-eye design often used as small panes over doorways in early homes. A second early method started with a blown cylinder of glass, sausage-shaped and several feet long. While still hot, the ends were cut off and the cylinder slit lengthwise and rolled flat. The crown glass has slightly circular spin marks and the cylinder glass is identified by slight wavy or bowed surfaces.

Windows and sash parts should be inspected for damage—joints may be loose, muntins split, or the frame rotted from exposure to weather. Open joints and splits can be repaired with exterior glue, wood dowels, or metal mending plates. Metal plates should be recessed slightly into the frame surface so they may later be hidden by filling, sanding,

and repainting. Badly rotted sections can sometimes be repaired by removing the damaged section and rebuilding with new wood or some of the modern exterior putties, which can be shaped and sanded like wood. New wood should be treated with a preservative such as penta for more permanent repairs, then carefully painted to match the surrounding window parts.

Reglazing old sash can be a delicate job. Wood parts may be dry and brittle; old glass is definitely fragile. Any loose putty should be removed back to where the putty is solidly attached to the sash frame. Broken panes are removed and replaced. Wear heavy gloves to protect your hands from glass splinters. A soldering iron with a flat tip will speed removal of hardened putty. The heat will soften stubborn putty so that you can scrape it free

Strong sun and harsh weather are particularly tough on window sills and parts. Annual inspection and maintenance and repair is required.

Photography: Lee Foster

Yearly touch-up of chipped areas will reduce water damage. Scrape away loose paint, sand carefully, prime and repaint surface when dry.

Photography: Bill Rooney

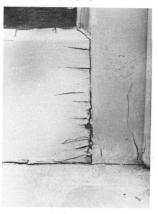

For top energy efficiency, windows must fit snugly. Loosened joints can be repaired with recessed metal mending plates screwed into place.

Badly damaged window joints may need to be gently separated, reglued with exterior adhesive, and tightly clamped together until dry.

with a putty knife or chisel. The putty must be removed down to the bare wood. As you go, remove and save the small metal glazier points. Pull them out with a pair of needle-nosed pliers.

Inspect your old replacement glass carefully. Determine the eye-level position on windows and place the more interesting glass here with the more ordinary glass for use in less noticeable areas. If you are lucky, the salvaged glass will be sized to fit your sash. Recutting antique glass is extremely difficult. If you are not familiar with the technique, let a professional do the cutting, and even then be prepared to lose some panes to breakage. Old glass is brittle.

Before inserting the glass in the sash, coat the muntins with a light brushing of linseed oil. This prevents the dry wood from draining oil out of the glazing compound. With your putty knife, lay down a thin layer of glazing compound along the rabbeted edge where the glass will sit. The glass should float in the glazing, not rest directly on the wood part. When the glass panes are pressed into place in the putty, insert the glazier's points to hold the pane in place. Be sure to drive the points deep enough into the wood so that they will later be covered with the final application of putty.

The glazing compound can be handled like children's modeling clay. Make a long rope or snake about 1/2-inch thick and press the putty along the window edges with your thumb. Now, holding the putty knife at a slight angle, draw it along the edge for a clean, straight line. If the knife sticks slightly, dip it in a little linseed oil for lubrication. Trim the putty corners at a bevel for a neat, professional-looking job. Allow the glazing compound to dry for several days before painting. Be sure to leave a slight paint edge on the glass to seal out the weather from the wood parts beneath.

Door repairs follow many of the same methods outlined for restoring windows. Splits and cracks are repaired with exterior glue and weatherproof nails or screws. Rotted sections are cut out and replaced with new wood or filled and shaped with exterior putties. To salvage an ornate wood front door, it may be worthwhile to consider using the newer epoxy resins injected through 1/2-inch holes in the door bottom to restore a badly decayed lower panel. Before trimming any door that scrapes in the frame, stop and inspect the hinges. Often loose hinges allow the door to hang out of square. Remove the hinge screws and check the soundness of the wood jamb. Perhaps nothing more than filling the holes with several glued toothpicks,

or drilling and installing wood dowels, will give you the sound wood needed to hold the hinge screws in place. If the door still sticks on the latch side, remove it and recess the hinge mortise about 1/8-inch on the jamb side. This will usually do the trick. If it still sticks, then the door must be planed to fit, but trimming the door itself should be your very last resort.

While repairing exterior doors, take a moment to inspect the thresholds. This is the part of the doorway that receives the most wear and exposure to the elements. If the threshold must be replaced, it may be necessary to gently pry off the door stop, remove nails or screws that hold the saddle in place and slide out the old threshold. If this is not possible, either try to split out the wood with a wide chisel or saw the threshold into three sections, remove the center, and work loose the two end pieces. Use the old section as a pattern for the new threshold, cut it to size, slide it into place, and fasten it securely. Coating the threshold with a wood preservative before you install it will extend its life.

Repairing Decorative Elements

Restoring decorative exterior components on an older home may range from the purely artistic and architectural parts, such as brackets, mouldings, ornate pediment

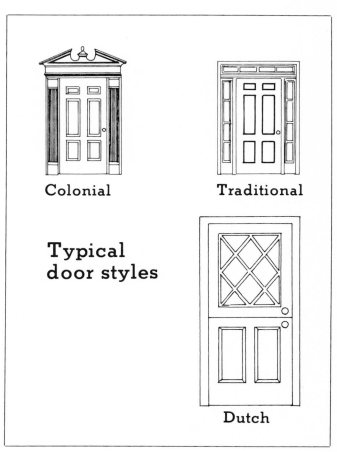

Colonial

Traditional

Typical door styles

Dutch

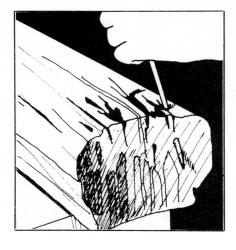

By using some of the newer, exterior epoxy and putty compounds, damaged wood parts can be repaired. First step requires removal of all rotted sections to sound wood.

The exterior filler can be brushed into cracks, or deeper areas can be filled with a putty knife. Deep repairs may require several applications to build up height.

When partially dry, the newer fillers can be shaped with a knife, plane, or a wood rasp. When sanded smooth, the surface should be primed and finished.

doorways, and gingerbread millwork, to decorative structural elements, such as porch and stair railings and support columns.

Artistic trim parts can be repaired similar to the techniques used on wood siding with exterior putty compounds. These fillers can be applied with a putty knife and before completely hardened, shaped with knife, chisel, wood rasp, and sandpaper. Once primed and finished, the repairs are inconspicuous. Missing parts can usually be recreated from patterns taken from existing pieces. A few pieces can be turned out by a local carpenter, usually of redwood or cedar, two easily worked and weather-resistant woods. A number of craftsmen now produce stock items based on the traditional designs or are equipped to manufacture special designs in limited quantities.

Before contacting craftsmen for custom work, be sure you have exhausted the possibility of finding the missing parts at a local salvage operation. The cost savings between used and newly created decorative parts can be dramatic.

Since safety as well as appearance is important, extra care should be taken when repairing decorative structural elements. A badly rotted porch deck should be replaced.

Most of the deck boards are vertical tongue and groove lumber. To remove parts of the decking without destroying the sound portion, locate the framing members underneath and be sure they are in solid condition. If not, they must be repaired before the deck is renovated. It is possible to prop up sagging piers and beams or strengthen timbers with extra steel or wood braces.

To remove deck boards, make a cut across the board so it falls directly over one half of the supporting framework with a sabre saw or chisel. Then, with a portable saw, rip the board up the middle avoiding the nails. Pry both halves loose and remove. If you are removing a number of boards, stagger the end cuts over several framing members so that your repair work blends later with the rest of the deck surface. Start replacing the new material by fitting the new tongue into the existing decking groove. Proceed until you have replaced all but the final deck board. Here, you will have to trim off the bottom half of the new deck groove so it will fit snugly onto the original deck board tongue. Be sure to use weather-resistant nails on all exterior repairs. Countersink nail heads and fill with exterior wood putty.

When making porch step repairs, inspect

the stair stringer, the side support piece, to see that it has not rotted out where it rests on the ground. Also determine that it is plumb and securely tied to the deck apron. Replacement stair treads should be vertical grain stepping, which wears better under heavy foot traffic and is stronger than flat grain lumber. The risers or vertical part of a step can be less expensive flat grain boards since they carry no real weight.

Wood columns, since they are structural as well as decorative, should be maintained in good repair. Condensation building up within the hollow columns causes deterioration from the inside. To prevent or correct this situation, vent holes should be drilled into the column about 6 inches from the top and the base. These vents allow air to circulate within the interior and prevent condensation from building up. The vent holes must remain open but should be covered with fine mesh screening to eliminate birds or wasps from building nests in the interior. Be careful not to clog the vent screening when painting the columns.

If the column base is deteriorated, it should be replaced as soon as possible. Either redwood or pressure-treated preservative wood is used. It will be necessary to jack

Below, a Victorian facade shows the decorative details that may need repair or replacement. In the West, redwood and cedar lumber is popular, in the South, cypress. All have natural weathering properties.

Photography: Val Hawes

Photography: Bill Rooney

Badly rotted column base, above, is too far gone to consider repair. Column must be raised, old base removed and replaced with sound wood. Note also that vent holes to column interior have been painted closed.

up the porch roof slightly, place a temporary support to hold it there, and remove the damaged column base. The new base is positioned, the column lowered, and the joint well caulked to prevent water seepage.

Some houses feature decorative metal trim—handrails, porch railings, window balconies, or ornate metal columns. Any rusted surfaces must be cleaned off down to the bare metal with wire brushes or emery cloth, a sandpaper made especially for metal work. Then the surface is coated with a metal primer and painted.

Wrought-iron metal parts can be repaired with rivets or spot welding. If you don't have the skills or equipment, a local metal working shop should be able to handle minor repairs for you. Cast-iron parts can be repaired, or new small sections created by using metal patching compounds. This clay-like material can be formed and shaped by hand, and when firm but not completely dry, can be further refined with a metal file or emery paper for a smooth finish.

Not all the wood and metal patching compounds mentioned in the exterior repair section will be available through your normal building materials supplier. However, if you use a little imagination, you can usually find a source for this material. For instance, a marine supply store or boat yard will usually have the necessary patching material to complete exterior wood repairs. For metal work, the local automotive supply house can provide metal filling and patching compounds as well as the rasps and files needed to shape the material. After all, rebuilding a dented fender is not that much different from recreating missing parts on a cast-iron trellis or porch column.

Under-eave peeling

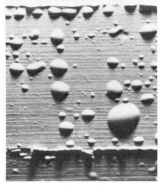

Blistering

Peeling

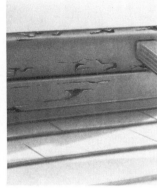

Peeling gutters and downspouts

Chalking

Checking

Alligatoring

Mildew

Exterior Finishes

No exterior finish can be any better than the surface to which it is applied. This means that a thorough preparation job is necessary if you hope to produce an attractive and durable exterior. The surface must be dry, clean and in sound condition. All siding and gutters, and downspouts should be repaired. Caulking should be applied around windows, doors, and trim boards. Nail heads should be countersunk and puttied.

If the wood surface is in poor condition, then the defects must be repaired before you

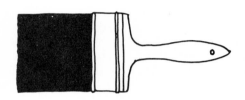

Types of brushes are as follows: **Wall** — widths from 3-6 inches with 4 inches the most common. Recommended for applying paint to broad surfaces such as walls, ceilings, siding.

Varnish/Enamel — widths from 1-3 inches. Generally used for applying varnish or enamel and designed for woodwork, doors, mouldings.

Sash/Trim — widths from 1-3 inches in three styles — flat, angular, and oval. The flat used for door and window sashes, the angular for precise edging, and the oval for narrow window mouldings and irregular surfaces, such as grille work or railings.

can expect to have a good paint job. Blistered and peeling paint should be scraped down to the bare wood with a stiff wire brush or paint scraper. Areas of scaling or alligatoring of old paint can be softened with a paste paint, removed, then scraped clean. Severe blistering or scaling usually indicates a moisture problem. It may be necessary to install small vent plugs to eliminate condensation problems within the walls.

All repaired areas should be sanded first with a coarse grade of paper and then with a finer grade to feather the edges from solid paint to the bare, stripped wood sections. All new or exposed wood should be primed with a coating compatible with the final or finish coat. Oil-based primer for oil paints, latex primer for water-based paints, metal primer for enamels on metal parts.

The average gallon of paint covers approximately 500 square feet of surface. To figure the amount of paint needed, measure the distance around the house foundation, the height from the foundation to the eaves, and estimate the area above on gable ends. Total the square footage of the house surface and divide by 500 to determine the approximate number of gallons required. Allow one gallon of trim paint for the average house, an extra gallon if you have an unusual amount of gingerbread and decorative trim.

If the surface is particularly dirty, wash it with a mild household detergent, hose it off, and allow the surface to dry if you are using oil-based paint. Latex can be applied to a slightly damp surface. Start your paint job at the highest point on the house and work downward. It may save you some excessive ladder moving if you paint the uppermost trim and siding at the same time. Use a small hanging platform on top of the ladder or hang your paint buckets from an "S" hook made of stiff wire.

Top-quality brushes or paint rollers are a good investment. They are easier to work with and eliminate the frustration of picking loose bristles from the fresh paint as too often happens with cheap brushes. Don't rush the job. Take the time to cover all surfaces uniformly, and carry a solvent soaked rag to wipe up any paint spills or drips. A large drop cloth under the work area will prevent paint drops from spotting shrubbery and walkways.

Ideally, you should plan your painting for clear dry weather with temperatures above 40 degrees. If possible, work in the shade rather than in direct sunlight. It is easier on you and allows the paint to soak in, instead of drying too rapidly on the wood surface.

If the house will be occupied while the painting is in progress, plan ahead so you can still accommodate normal family activities. Paint one access door first so it has time to dry before you reach other doors. Paint one half of the porch first and the second half later. On outside steps, paint alternate treads so at least you can giant-step your way in and out of the house while the paint dries.

Be sure to cover all surfaces, the tops and bottoms of doors and windows, the underside of step overhangs, and the bottom edge of siding and foundation trim boards. Metal parts are usually painted last. And make sure you treat all surfaces. The underside of metal railings collects rain water and therefore needs special protection.

Before you put the ladder and brushes away, walk around the house for a final inspection. Then clean all paint equipment, pick up the drop cloths, and congratulate yourself on completion of a major part of your restoration project.

Finding the right exterior paint color combination may take a little experimentation. Use your research as a guide, then reproduce a black and white photo on a copy machine. Use colored pencils or pens to try several combinations until you develop the best mix.

Photography: Norman Prince

Chapter 7
Interior Restoration

The interior treatment is usually the heart and soul of any restoration project. Here is where you and your family will spend most of your time; here is where you will entertain your friends and show off the hours of detailed labor devoted to reconstructing a period atmosphere. The approach you take to interior work may lead to the success or failure of the entire project.

By this time you should have developed detailed plans and have a firm idea of what the finished interior will look like. It may take you several years to complete all the detailed work, do the fussy hand finishing, obtain and install the missing parts, and furnish the interior to your satisfaction. Dreams don't come quickly or easily, but if you have your ultimate goal in mind, then completion of each segment is a minor victory along the way.

And minor victories will become important as the job progresses. At times the project may seem overwhelming and impossible to complete as originally planned. Financing may run short, key materials may be late in delivery or difficult to locate, unexpected problems will arise, and the hundreds of daily decisions become mind-boggling. But with perseverance and dedication plus a streak of selfish stubbornness, you can see it through to completion. You may not always want to go through the experience again but your successful restoration project will establish a satisfying sense of pride and accomplishment in you and your family.

Before you begin actual work on the interior, you or your architect should sit down with the contractor and his work force to explain in detail just how the project will progress. Use the list you developed to make sure all understand why some items must be

In Atlanta, Georgia, an 1890 restored home features original, deep relief-carved wood mouldings. The millwork was heavily varnished, but the new owners decided on an off-white paint for contrast.

Photography: Steve Hogben

completed before others are started, how the work must be done, and what items are to be repaired, replaced, or added. Explain why you are willing to compromise in some areas but insist on holding to accurate historical principles in other sections. Get everyone totally involved in the spirit of this restoration right from the start. Establish one individual as the source for all final decisions and stick with your original plan as long as possible. Unforeseen problems will invariably pop up, but they should be solved as quickly as possible so you can immediately return to your planned schedule.

Assign one area in the house as the storage location for materials and parts and make sure all know the disposition of any items that are removed as the work progresses. Some will be salvaged and should be stored in one safe location until they are needed, other materials will be thrown out. A large drop box should be scheduled to handle all trash and emptied at regular intervals so that additional material can be added as it develops. Any restoration project generates a surprisingly large material flow—lumber, plywood, and drywall panels arriving, broken plaster, lath, and damaged wood parts leaving. Plan your traffic flow carefully to eliminate excessive material underfoot in the work areas.

Based on the experience of other families who have traveled the residential restoration route, the following suggestions will save you energy, time and money, and eliminate a lot of misunderstanding and hard feelings during the interior work.

1. Stagger delivery schedules so that a minimum amount of material is on hand at one time. This will reduce confusion and possible damage. Items should arrive when they are ready for installation rather than weeks ahead of time. This is particularly important if you are not living in the house during construction. It reduces the chance of vandalism or theft on an unprotected project.

2. Use small pieces of masking tape and a felt pen to label items that are to remain or be disposed of throughout the house. Parts to be removed and reused should be marked as to the new location. "Salvage—reuse in front hall." These road signs only take a few minutes to apply and can save a lot of grief.

3. Protect everything possible. Remove any hardware, lighting fixtures, or mirrors that might be damaged. Raise low-hanging chandeliers to ceiling height for free access beneath. Remove doors from high traffic lanes and apply a big "X" of masking tape to windows so workers will be discouraged from backing a long length of lumber through them.

4. Let the workmen know what habits you expect from them. Unfortunately, most are used to working in the rough carpentry surroundings of new construction. They think nothing of grinding out a cigarette under their heel on the floor, making pencil notations on the walls, dropping material on the floor, or leaning them against the walls. Plumbers are notorious for setting up their pipe-cutting and threading machines and dropping metal chips and oil all over the floor. Establish some do's and don'ts right up front. The workers must conform to all guidelines that you set.

5. Even if you intend to refinish the floors, cover them with building paper taped in place. Any tile work, counters, or floors should be covered, and protect the enamel finish on basins and tubs by applying paper with a flour and water paste. It is easily removed at a later and safer time.

6. Drop cloths or inexpensive plastic sheets are a must to protect surfaces from paint spatter or wet plaster drops. Drape them over mantels, window seats, wall and ceiling fixtures as well as all floor areas. Several large cloths can be moved from room to room as you proceed. Drop cloths will more than pay for themselves in reducing damage and cleanup time.

7. Identify and protect your tools. A splash of orange spray paint or your initials or driver's license number etched into your tools with an engraving tip will avoid a lot of misunderstanding with the workmen. For security, have a tool box or cabinet where you can lock up the tools when not in use.

Basement Repairs

It is probably wise to start your interior work in the basement in order to correct any moisture or structural problems that may affect other parts of the house. These two important items should be solved first before you attempt any other repairs.

Basement moisture can be generated from within or be entering from outside through the walls. Inside, condensation is the major moisture contributor. Warm, moist air condenses into water beads when it comes in contact with a cool surface. Storm windows on the basement openings will help prevent the problem. Covering old water pipes with layers of fiberglass or foam plastic insulation and installing a dehumidifier system will reduce the sweating situation. In 24 hours, a good humidifier will subtract more than a gallon of water from the surrounding air.

Moisture entering through the outside walls may be coming through holes or cracks in the wall surface. Try to fix the leaks from the inside. If this is not successful, then you are faced with the difficult job of waterproofing the outside wall surface. If water appears to be entering through inside holes punctured through concrete or cinder block walls, the repairs are fairly simple. With a chisel, undercut the opening and brush out any dust or loose particles. Mix up a plug of quick-setting hydraulic cement, force it into the hole, allow it to set slightly and smooth the surface with a hand trowel before the cement completely hardens. Any cracks wider than 1/8 inch must be chiseled wider at the back than the wall surface. This wedge shape opening keeps the patching material from falling out. Cement mortar or two-part epoxy mix can be used to repair wall cracks. Follow directions supplied with either material. If moisture seems to be entering through the surface of a porous wall, then the entire surface must be waterproofed. Brush down the wall to remove any loose particles, then hose it off lightly to dampen the surface. A commercial waterproofing compound is then applied with a stiff brush, rubbing the compound into all small cracks and holes. For best results, follow in 24 hours with a second coat of the compound.

When inside repairs don't solve a damp basement, then you must attack the problem from outside. Several coats of black mastic waterproofing compound are scrubbed into the outside wall, and drain tiles, running parallel to the foundation, are installed to carry off surface water to a dry well or storm sewer. The excavation should be backfilled to within a foot of the surface with gravel for improved drainage. A professional basement waterproofing company may be less expen-

The surface of concrete or cinder block basement walls must be thoroughly cleaned before waterproofing repairs begin. Wire brush by hand or power drill to remove loose paint, efflorescence, dirt and grease.

Chisel out all holes, cracks and joints wider at the back than at wall surface to create a wedge-shaped opening. This helps lock hydraulic cement or epoxy mix into place to assure tight fitting repairs.

To seal entire wall surface, dampen area, then brush on a heavy coat of commercial waterproofing compound. Apply with a stiff brush, rubbing the compound into all the small cracks and holes. Then recoat in 24-hours.

Large holes may require several layers of patching material to build up proper depth. If interior repairs don't solve the problem, drain tile and several coats of black waterproofing are applied to outside walls.

Photography: Leo Pinard

Since beams and timbers support the house structure, repairs and leveling must be completed before other interior work begins. Floor jacks, wood shims and cross bracing will correct sagging and squeaking floors.

sive in the long run. The commercial technique calls for sealing the wall from the inside with a thick epoxy coating, then pumping a sealing compound under pressure through the earth close to the outside wall. The compound seeps down the wall, hardens and seals the wall from water penetration.

While you are in the basement, inspect the major beams and timbers supporting the floor structure above. Sagging beams create uneven and squeaking floors, cause windows and doors to stick, plaster walls and ceilings to crack and even promote roof leaks. In most construction found in older houses, any sag in the first floor affects the entire structure. To correct sagging floors, the supporting floor joist must be raised back to their original position. A short screw-type house jack with a 4x4 post on top and a heavy beam spanning the joist, or an adjustable jack post are used. These are both powerful instruments capable of lifting over 12,000 pounds. They are easy to operate but must be used with care. Don't attempt to hurry the floor leveling job. Once the jack is in position, rotate the handle to raise the beam against the floor joist. As soon as resistance builds up, stop. The floor structure must have time to adjust to the leveling pressure. Take no more than a 1/4 or 1/2 turn of the jack handle every 24 hours. It may take a week or more but the job can't be rushed or you will create more damage than you are correcting. Once the floor is level, install lally columns or steel jack posts at each end of the supporting beam.

Squeaking floors can be repaired from the surface or from the underside, and in severe cases, you may have to do both. All loose floorboards should be renailed. Once

squeaks are located, angle drill small pilot holes and use special ring-shanked flooring nails to tighten joints. The combination of angle nailing and annular-ringed nails provides a secure fastening. If the basement ceiling is open, tap shingle wedges between any loose joist and the subfloor. For stubborn squeaks, it may be necessary to drill through the subfloor and use wood screws to draw the flooring down tightly.

While in the basement, inspect the diagonal bracing between the floor joist. This bridging prevents the joist from warping and creating floor squeaks. All loose bridging should be renailed, and if for some reason your house is without this bracing, it should be installed. Use either solid 2x8 sections cut to fit between the joist and toenailed in place, or 2x4 material for cross-bridging.

Once the moisture and structural problems are solved, you are ready to tackle any other major changes before you begin the finish work. If your plans call for drastic changes in the floor plan, be sure to locate and identify any bearing walls before you start cutting holes for doors or dismantling wall sections. These key structural elements of the house carry part of the load of floors above. They run perpendicular to the floor joist, and extreme caution should be exercised before disturbing any load-bearing partition. Check with your architect, contractor, or building inspector before tampering

Stairways are potential danger spots that require careful inspection. For safety's sake, treads must be solid and tight, bannisters and railings replaced or repaired, and adequate lighting installed.

Photography: WGBH, Boston

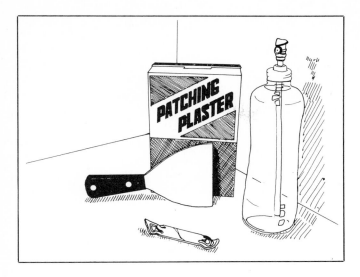

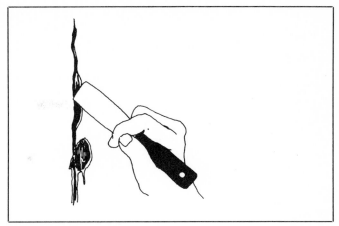

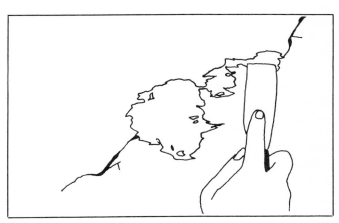

Above, tools for plaster wall repairs include a flexible putty knife, beer can opener to remove loose material and undercut crack opening, spray bottle to dampen area, plaster mix or patching compound.

Above right, fine cracks and nail holes can be filled with ready-to-use latex patching material. Use your finger to force material into cracks or corners, and smooth paste into joints with a putty knife.

Right, filling larger cracks requires undercutting opening to an inverted V-shape for anchorage. Remove excess and smooth surface with putty knife. Lightly sandpaper surface when dry, then prime and paint.

with the structural integrity of the house.

For safety's sake, the stairs throughout the home require careful inspection. Since they carry a significant amount of weight and are subjected to vibration, repairs should be made with screws and glue rather than nails. All wedges should be driven tightly into place and glued. Loose treads and risers need to be repaired, and badly damaged treads replaced. To eliminate stair squeaks, install additional support on the center stair stringer, install glue blocks screwed into place where the risers meet the treads, and retack any loose carpet runners on the stairs.

Older homes present opportunities for creating extra storage space. Pantry walls can be removed to enlarge a kitchen area, shallow storage can be cut into walls between the studs and closets, drawers or extra shelving may be built into the underside of stairways. If you discover a dumbwaiter in your older home, it can usually be rebuilt into a closet, or partitioned off for built-in drawers or bookcases. If it runs through several floor levels, a dumbwaiter can be converted into a clothes chute, collecting dirty jeans from the upstairs bedrooms and funneling them to the laundry in the basement. Check your local building codes carefully.

Most require that any opening that runs through several floor levels be lined with fireproof material.

Plaster Repair

With the major structural repairs completed, you can turn your attention to preparing the ceilings and walls for the final decorative finishes. In making plaster repairs, do the ceiling first, then the walls. This eliminates any chance of damaging freshly repaired walls when moving ladders about to work on the ceiling. Since the chemicals in plaster will "burn" or stain wood floors, be sure to spread drop cloths about the room for maximum protection.

Hairline cracks on the ceiling and around windows and doors can be filled with putty, spackle, or wood dough. Remove any loose particles from the crack, dampen slightly and rub the filler across the crack with a putty knife or finger, forcing the material into the opening. Larger cracks must be enlarged and undercut to provide a grip for the filler. Professional tools are available for this work but an ordinary beer can opener will do the job. Using the point, drag it along the crack to dislodge any loose material, undercut the opening, and dampen the area before applying the filler. A wet paintbrush, plant atomizer, or empty window spray cleaner bottle is handy.

Small holes, caused by furniture dents, slamming door knobs, or rambunctious children require a little different approach. Here, on holes up to a foot in diameter, you will be placing the plaster directly on the lath attached to the wall studs. Recent houses will have wire mesh or metal lath, older houses used rough-sawn wooden lath, and earlier homes may display handsplit wood lath. You may also find evidence of plaster mixed with horse hair or hemp-like fibers as a binder in older walls.

If the lath is still in good shape, follow the recommendations for undercutting the edges and dampening the perimeter plaster. With a putty knife apply the first coat of plaster to the hole, forcing in the material deep enough to flow through and around the lath. This locks the new plaster to the wall. Apply a first coat about 1/4-inch thick and let it dry. Then spread a second coat to level out the wall. When the lath is damaged, don't bother repairing it. Instead, cut a piece of wire mesh several inches larger, all around, than the hole and thread a piece of wire through the middle. Holding onto the wire, roll the mesh until it is small enough to fit into the hole and open up behind the wall. Lay a ruler, dowel, or small wood stick across the hole, bridging from one side to the other. Twist the wire around the dowel, locking the mesh into place. Plaster the hole as explained, cutting or removing the wire between the first and second plaster application. Water-damaged plaster on the ceiling or walls must be removed back to solid plaster areas. The water usually turns the plaster spongy and dissolves the plaster key behind the lath, leaving the surface floating loose from the backing. Remove the rotted plaster in chunks and, when you reach the solid portion, undercut slightly before making repairs.

Resurfacing large plaster areas is a difficult task for beginners. You need a large mortarboard to mix several plaster bags at one time, and the experience to get the proper consistency, particularly when working overhead on ceiling repairs. Without professional tools like hawks, floats, and large straightedges, the average homeowner can be in trouble. Some of this equipment can be rented but large plaster work is generally better left to the professionals.

To finish off plaster repairs, the surface should be smoothed with fine sandpaper, feathering the edges around the hole to blend with the surrounding wall. In some instances, you don't want a smooth patch. Nothing stands out more than a smooth plaster patch on a textured wall. In this case, before the plaster dries, daub a wet sponge onto the repaired surface to produce a slight texture. Wire mesh screening wrapped around a small wood block, or a whisk broom, can be used to recreate patterns on a textured plaster wall surface.

Before you attempt to paint over a plaster repair, the surface must be primed to seal the new plaster. Shellac, sealer, or paint can be used as a primer.

If decorative plaster mouldings or ceiling medallions have been damaged, repair or replacement is possible. Small broken sections that have been salvaged can be fixed back in place with quick-setting glues. Larger decorative sections can be rebuilt with fresh plaster, which is carefully shaped while still damp, and when dry, further touched up with small chisels, knives, files, and sandpaper. With a little artistic talent, the new section will be almost a perfect match when painted.

Longer sections of damaged or missing

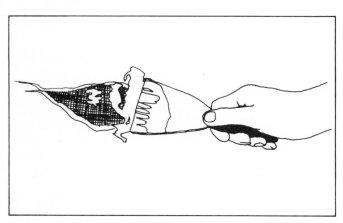

Large holes, broken through the plaster, require special treatment. Clean out the old plaster, undercut edges and tack or staple wire screen to the lath to anchor plaster. Large holes need second application.

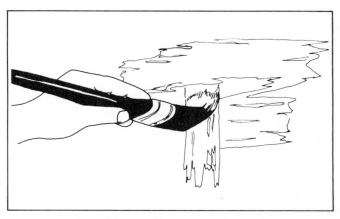

When plaster patched surfaces are thoroughly dry and smooth, they should be spot primed with the same paint you have selected for a finish coat. Directions on the label will indicate if prime coat should be thinned.

Photography: Cumberland Woodcraft Co.

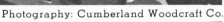

Photography: Bendix Mouldings

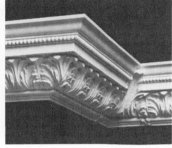

Photography: Focal Point Inc.

Photography: Focal Point Inc.

Restoration activity has revived the manufacture of period decorations. Above, a selection of Victorian mill-work for interior and exterior repairs; ornate plaster cornice reproductions and carved wood period de-signs. Wall or ceiling medallion, dome rims in several styles, and sunburst arch illustrate prefabricated decorative elements now available. Many resemble plaster but are made of tougher synthetic material.

plaster mouldings can sometimes be replaced by duplicating the pattern with stock wood mouldings which, when painted, will match the plaster profile. If this is not possible, you can usually make a mold or die to recreate the decorative plaster mouldings. Select a short section of good moulding and coat it liberally with vegetable shortening to act as a release agent. Then a large handful of wet plaster is run across the pattern to shape itself to the moulding profile. Remove the mold and let it dry completely. Coat the inside surface of the dry mold with shortening, apply wet plaster to the area of the missing moulding and run the mold over this surface to reproduce the profile on the missing section. Remove the excess plaster and smooth the surface with a wet brush.

Ceiling medallions, ornate mouldings, and cornices in traditional historical patterns are available from several supply sources. Some are recreated in plaster or synthetic materials and are easily glued into place. This provides a quick and relatively inexpensive method of decorating the ceiling and upper wall areas.

Window Repairs

Windows are perhaps the most demanding elements in a restoration project, yet offer the best satisfaction for the time involved. From both inside and outside, windows set the tone and establish the personality of the home. From a practical standpoint, they must operate efficiently to provide light, insulation, security, and ventilation. Aesthetically, light streaming through the bubbles and swirls of old glass, or adding splashes of color as it enters through stained glass windows creates a touch of nostalgia to any interior. Beveled and cut glass produces a rainbow effect as light is split into colors passing through the window prisms.

Ornate glasswork reached its height around the turn of the century and declined after 1910, when mass production began to take over. The intricate and complex designs of the Art Nouveau period, 1880-1910, gave way to the more standard patterns of the Art Deco movement in the 1920s and 30s.

When shopping for old stained glass at an antique store or salvage yard, always take the window into the clear sunlight for a close

109

inspection. More valuable hand-blown glass is often uneven in thickness, and one side may be relatively smooth, the other rippled. Quality, thick glass with beveled edges, called jewels, has a prismatic effect dividing the light rays into colors. Machine-made glass is uniform in thickness and texture. Machine pressed jewels have a more uniform surface and usually don't create a prismatic effect. Any designs on the glass surface should be etched or painted by hand and fired into the glass, rather than screened or brushed onto the surface.

The cost of repairing old glass windows is usually expensive. A sag or bulge, hairline cracks, or loose lead joints are fairly simple to correct. However, badly damaged or missing pieces of hand-blown glass require the services of an expert for proper repair and precision matching of missing parts. But most restorers agree the cost and effort are worth the trouble. Ornate glasswork over the front door or built into the sidelights, or perhaps a spectacular stained glass window on the stair landing, adds a tremendous impact to any old home. Protect your investment in old glass by having a special rider added to your household insurance policy to cover loss and repair of leaded, stained, and cut glass windows.

If windows in an older house stick or are painted shut, don't assume there is nothing you can do to correct the situation. You can and should make them operable again. Through years of neglect and sloppy maintenance, freeing painted-shut windows requires a little work. You may have to make corrections from both inside and outside the window. With a sharp knife or razor blade, slit the paint seal between the window frame and the sash. Then gently tap a wide putty knife blade into the joint. This should free the window, but for stubborn situations you may need to use a small pry bar or wide wood chisel to apply added leverage. Once the window is free, scrape out any dirt or dried paint from the side stops or bottom rabbet. Sand these areas lightly for a smooth working window.

If the window sash is bowed or expanded from moisture, it may be necessary to remove the sash from the frame. Carefully pry off the stop moulding and remove the sash. Clean out and sand the sash track or channel, and in severe cases, plane down the sash sides for a more comfortable fit.

In the majority of older houses, double-hung windows were the most popular style. The sash rode in twin channels so that the bottom sash could be raised and the top sash lowered to provide ventilation. For ease of operation, the sashes were counterbalanced

You may need professional assistance in restoring and repairing ornate stained glass panels. Vibration from slamming doors or a settling foundation may create sags, hairline cracks in glass or loose lead joints.

Photography: Steve Marley

Traditional period millwork parts are being reproduced today by a number of small, local craftsmen. Below, the typical wood, Colonial double-hung window features "6 over 9" glass panes, and moulded wood casing.

Photography: National Woodwork Mfrs. Assn.

with sash weights, sausage-shaped cast-iron weights, supported by cords over a pulley.

In time, the sash cord became frayed or rotted, and broke. To gain repair access on some double-hung windows, it is necessary to pry off the window casing moulding or frame to expose the weights in the wall behind the window side jamb. In other windows there is a small pocket or door on the jamb side attached with screws. Remove the sash and unscrew the pocket cover to reach inside. In either case, once the weights are exposed, the repair is simple. Replace the old cord with new cord, or substitute sash chain for a longer lasting repair.

Solid brass was often used on original window hardware. It is worthwhile to brighten the hinges, latches, casement arms, and locks with metal polish or fine steel wool, then protect the new look with a spray coat of lacquer. Be sure all screws are retightened and the window operates smoothly.

There is a definite sequence recommended when painting windows. In general, start from the middle and work out; from the top and work down. Paint the muntins, the interior wood parts holding the panes, first. Then the horizontal sash parts top and bottom, the vertical sash sides, and finally, the window frame itself. Work quickly so that the paint does not dry before the adjoining section is painted. Be sure to seal the top, bottom, and both sides of the sash.

Double-hung windows, where one sash slides behind another, follow the same paint plan but take a little more thought. Begin by raising the bottom sash and lowering the top one until the bottom of the upper sash is exposed at the meeting or lock rail. Paint the bottom section of the outside window first, then slide the sash back to a near normal position and proceed with the painting. Avoid painting the windows shut; casement and awning windows should be left slightly open to dry, and double-hung windows should be raised and lowered before completely dry to prevent sticking. When the windows are dry, apply a small amount of silicone spray or paraffin wax to help the windows operate freely.

Door Repair

There are few things in a house more annoying than a door that won't work properly—either it won't close or it sticks shut, the latch bolt won't engage the strike plate or the bolt won't move at all, the handle is loose or the door bottom scrapes the rug. As annoying as these may be, they are all easy repair projects.

Before attempting any planing of the door to fit the opening, refer to the door repair section in the chapter on Exterior Restoration for suggestions on resetting the hinges to correct this situation. If the door is slightly bowed, it is usually much easier to remove and reposition the stop moulding than trying to correct the bow. To trim the door bottom for rug clearance, take off the minimum amount needed to do the job. A door with a big gap at the floor line looks like a fast-growing 11-year-old with his pants'

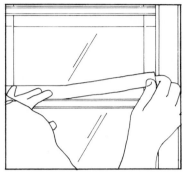

Once window repairs are completed and units operate freely, they should be protected with several coats of quality paint. Make the job easier by applying masking tape along each window pane edge before any painting begins.

Properly painting a double-hung window calls for pre-planning. Begin by raising the inside sash and lowering the outside sash. Paint the inside sash, first the mullions, then the frame. Do not paint the top edge until later.

Next paint the outside sash—mullions, then frame—but do not paint the bottom edge. Move the sash back to one inch from their closed position, and paint exposed parts. Finally, paint the window casing and sill.

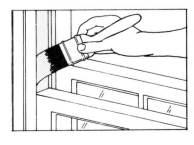

When the paint is dry, move both sashes as far as they will go in the closed position. Paint the upper jambs. When this is dry, raise both sash and paint the lower jambs. Remove masking tape and inspect your job thoroughly.

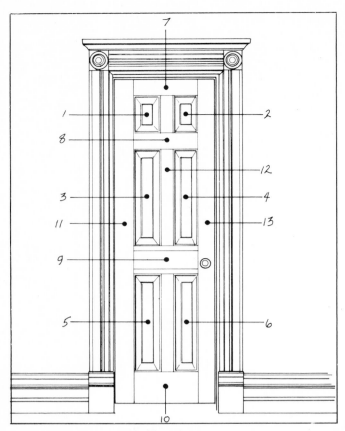

Because of the three-dimensional construction, panel doors should be painted in sequence to avoid paint runs and brush strokes. Start with the interior panels and moulding, working from the top to bottom. Then, starting at the top, paint the horizontal dividing rails and then the vertical stiles. Finally, both long edges, and top and bottom edges.

for a broken one. Most of the early mortise locks were made up of cast-iron components. If any of these parts are broken, they are virtually impossible to repair. Try to find a replacement lock at a junk or salvage yard. As a last resort, steal a lock from your upstairs bedroom closet door and replace it with a new one. When the latch bolt will not engage the strike plate on the jamb, take the easy way out. Rather than trying to rehang the entire door, remove and install the strike plate a little bit lower. Chisel out the jamb for the new position and use a bit of wood putty to fill the slight hole above.

Like windows, panel doors must be painted in a strict sequence to avoid paint runs and uneven brush strokes. The system basically follows the way the door was made and the wood grain of the various parts. Start on the inside of the door, painting the top two panels and their moulding, then the middle and bottom pair of panels. Return to the top and paint the horizontal rails across, down to the bottom. Then paint the vertical stiles, moving from the left to the right. Be sure to catch the top and bottom door edges. Although no one ever sees these surfaces, the paint acts as a seal to prevent moisture absorption through the end grain of the stiles.

Refinishing Millwork

Like your exterior finish, the final appearance of your interior millwork can be no better than the surface to which you apply the stain or paint. In fact, since your family and friends will have the opportunity to inspect your handiwork close up, you should take extra pains in preparing all of the interior surfaces.

First, make all necessary millwork repairs and replacements. All loose mouldings should be renailed. You can avoid splitting the wood at the end of boards, particularly in hard woods, if you predrill a small hole before inserting the finish nail. Countersink all nail heads slightly below the surface and fill with spackle or wood putty. Dents and gouges should be filled and sanded smoothly. Any gaps or joints where one piece of moulding meets another require filling. Chipped, scratched, or flaking paint surfaces are sanded with a fine grade of paper, feathering the edge smoothly back to where the paint is in good condition. Prime all fill spots and raw wood before applying the finish paint coat.

Make a tour of each room, checking each section of millwork as you go—mouldings tight and well-sanded, wainscot and paneling nailed in place, steps, balusters, and handrails securely fastened. Inspect the

cuffs up around his shins. To reduce splintering when you plane or saw across the grain on the outside edge or stile, score your cut lines on both sides with a sharp knife.

Any splits in the door should be opened slightly, filled with glue and clamped closed. Long screws, countersunk and filled, or wood dowels applied with glue, will strengthen repairs. Loose panels in a door, however, should *not* be nailed or glued in place. They were originally installed in the frame channel to float slightly so that there is a small movement allowed as the wood expands and contracts due to changes in the temperature and humidity conditions.

Mechanical problems with the handle, latch, or strike plate need careful inspection. If the latch bolt will not move when the handle is turned, it may be painted in position. A little scraping should free it. If it still will not move, then the spring inside the mortise lock is either dislodged or broken. Remove the handle and escutcheon plate, and unscrew the lock from the door edge. Open it up and check the spring inside. Reposition a loose spring or get a replacement doors and windows and the frames surrounding them, trim around the fireplaces and mantels and the wall mouldings at the ceiling and floor lines.

Should you recoat the existing finish or should you strip the original finish down to the bare wood? There is no pat answer to this question. The decision depends upon your personal taste, the research that may indicate how the surface was originally treated, and the present condition of the paint or clear finish, and the quality, grain, and condition of the wood itself.

It is easier to make a decision on naturally finished wood. At least you can see through the relatively clear varnish, shellac, lacquer, or stain to determine the type and quality of the wood beneath. Some woods are easily identified by their grain configurations and colors—the strong, dominant pattern of oak, the dark, close pores of American walnut, and the rich warmth of fine mahogany. However, earlier craftsmen were adept at using more common woods, and sometimes hickory or pecan was stained to resemble walnut, tupelo, magnolia, or birch treated to produce a cherry appearance. Some highly figured woods were actually bland, grainless material carefully finished and grained with combs, feathers and stamps to resemble the swirls, knots, and patterns of fine hardwoods.

To determine just what wood you are working with, take a small knife and scrape away the finish in an inconspicuous spot— mouldings behind a door, the top of raised millwork on a fireplace front above eye level. Don't be surprised at what you uncover; raw walnut is a dull gray-brown, cherry a light tan, and mahogany a pale pink.

If the wood appears to be quality material, if the finish is in poor shape and if major repairs or extensive replacement of raw wood parts is needed, it is probably wise to strip the finish completely. However, if the existing finish is in good condition and free from repairs and replacement parts, then you might try amalgamation, a trick known to the experienced wood finishers.

The amalgamation process is nothing more than a softening and redistribution of the existing finish, which hides the scratches and minor imperfections of any old surface without losing the soft patina built up through the years. Start by washing down the surface with a mild detergent to remove dirt, grime, and fingerprints. Then, if the original varnish, shellac, or lacquer appears to have been polished with wax, wipe down the surface with a rag dampened with a little turpentine to remove the wax buildup.

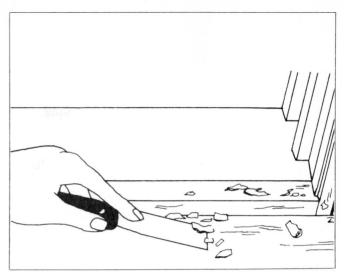

Stripping interior painted or varnished surfaces is a messy and time consuming task. First scrape off any loose finish with a putty knife then apply chemical paint remover, sand, prime and finish.

Whatever the finish, the amalgamation process is the same. For shellac, use denatured alcohol; varnish and lacquer have their own thinning solvents. Place a little solvent on a clean cloth pad and rub the finished surface in a circular motion. Go lightly until the finish just begins to dissolve, then complete the small area by wiping in the grain direction. Do one small section at a time, melting and spreading the old finish.

The question of how to handle painted surfaces demands a little more detective work. You should scrape the paint away in several areas to determine the type and quality of the wood. Don't be disappointed to discover some pretty ordinary species were used to construct ornate paneled doors and fancy fireplace decorations.

If, after investigation, you decide to strip clear finished or painted surfaces, the job is relatively easy but time-consuming and messy. You might scrape and sand to remove the old finish, but a chemical remover is quicker and safer on the wood. Removers are available in liquid form or in a heavy-body paste or cream. On vertical surfaces, the thicker paste will cling to the surface long enough to become effective.

In stripping paint or clear finishes, it is easiest if all hardware is first removed. Unscrew door handles and escutcheon plates, hinges and catches wherever possible. This will speed the stripping, since you won't have to work around hardware in place, and protects the metal from chemical reaction to the remover. Where hardware cannot be removed, cover the metal with masking tape or apply a protective coating of petroleum jelly. You'll find it more convenient to remove doors from the frames and set them up on saw horses. Now you can apply the remover to a horizontal surface and work at a much more comfortable height.

Since some removers contain fairly harsh chemicals, wear rubber gloves and glasses or goggles for hand and eye protection. Work in a well-ventilated room to dispel the strong odors. Use a natural bristle brush and flood the remover onto the surface. Work an area no more than several feet square at one time. Let the remover do most of the work for you, put it on in a thick layer and keep it wet. As the surface begins to soften, the old finish can be scraped or lifted off with a putty knife. It will take about five minutes for the remover to blister the surface finish, then scrape with the wood grain when possible. If you are working through an old finish of several coats, a second application may be needed.

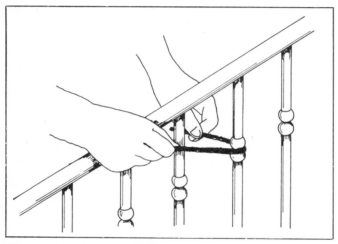

When stripping finish from ornate turnings and detailed millwork on stairways and furniture, try an old tooth brush or steel wool twisted into a string to remove finish from crevices and small joints.

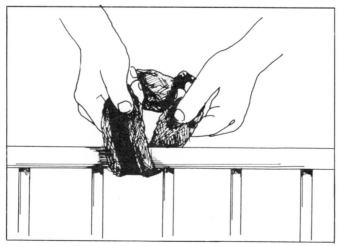

Broader, rounded surfaces require a different treatment. Several strips of tape on the back of steel wool increase its effectiveness. Hold both ends and pull back and forth like a shoe shine rag to clean rounded surfaces.

Flat surfaces are stripped quickly, but ornately carved or turned wood parts need special attention. Flood the carvings with remover and brush the chemical into deep cracks with a small bristle brush or old toothbrush. As the remover begins to work, use steel wool, nut picks, fingernail file, or nails to clean out the crevices. In oak or other open-pored wood it is necessary to get as much of the paint or finish out of the pores as possible. Dip a piece of steel wool into the remover and scrub with hard pressure.

For round surfaces such as columns, newel posts, and rail spindles, use burlap or steel wool where a flat putty knife is not effective. A small strand of burlap or coarse twine soaked in the remover can be wrapped around curved pieces and "sawn" back and forth like a shoe-shine rag to clean out the narrow openings in turned wood parts.

Inspect your work carefully and reapply the remover; scrape or use steel wool on any stubborn spots. Once the original finish is completely stripped, you must neutralize the chemicals absorbed by the wood before you consider applying a new finish. Use steel wool soaked in turpentine or lacquer thinner to wash down the wood surface, working with the grain. To complete the stripping job, clean your brushes and scrapers immediately, collect the burlap and steel wool, and dispose of the gunky remover and other waste before they can create a fire hazard. Many of the chemicals are inflammable and should be removed from the house at the first opportunity.

Final Finishes

Now that the drudgery of repair and stripping are behind you, a variety of wood finishes are available to help you create the exact period look you've had in mind for these many months. If you want the beauty of natural wood grain to show, you can choose from an array of varnishes, lacquers, and shellacs that leave a protective film on top of the wood surface. Penetrating finishes, those which sink into the wood structure for a three-dimensional treatment, include the traditional boiled linseed oil or the newer tung oil, polymer or polyurethane clear or stain finishes. Then there are the pure stains, oil, dye, and alcohol soluable, which are usually protected with a coat or two of clear finish. Now add in the various opaque finishes, oil, or water-based paints in flat, semigloss, and enamel treatments, and complete the list with several of the unique finishes popular with the old-time craftsmen such as fumed oak, marbleizing, and wood-grain simulations. The options are many.

Photography: Wood Moulding and Millwork Producers

The authenticity added by moulding and millwork details is well worth the time involved. Above, a formal living room gains personality through careful detailing and raised panels of the fireplace and mantel.

In contrast, the simple country interior shown above, employs ceiling cornice and chair rail mouldings to relieve plain white walls. Buggy seat and pine paneled corner cabinet round out the feeling.

Your decision will not be as difficult as it might first appear. Based on your historical research and your personal taste, many possibilities can quickly be eliminated. If you favor natural wood finishes, be careful not to have too much of a good thing. Just as a completely painted interior can be sterile, a room of nothing but wood grain can be monotonous. Perhaps the best balance will include both natural and painted surfaces with each complementing the other.

Most of the finishes can be applied by any restorer with average skills. Fumed oak may be an exception. This process exposes the wood to strong ammonia fumes in a sealed chamber and results in a somewhat drab, graying effect. There are probably not more than a handful of old-time experts who understand the mysteries of temperature, humidity, types of oak, and exposure of deadly ammonia fumes to produce a given effect. Marbleizing kits, some applied with vacuum-cleaner spray attachments, and wood-graining kits with special brushes, glaze, and graining pads can produce surprisingly professional results with a little practice.

Although most finishes can be used by the homeowner, you may need some professional advice when it comes to particulars. For instance, if you are starting with raw oak wood and wish to achieve a dark, stained finish, you will need to fill the large oak pores with the proper filler, apply the correct stain

and protect your efforts with a two-coat finish. Depending on the temperature and humidity and the type of materials used, you will need certain brushes and use different techniques and drying times. You may have to sand between coats, and you must be sure that all three basic items are chemically compatible with each other. Obtaining a long-lasting wood finish that highlights the depth and beauty of wood grain is an art.

When shopping for finishing materials, avoid the building discount centers and work directly with knowledgeable personnel and a professional paint supply house. Prices will be basically the same, and the additional information and help you will receive will be invaluable. You can also increase your talents along the way. Your public library or local bookstore offers a selection of volumes full of finishing ideas, illustrations, warnings, and tips. Some are under the home repair section, but seek out several good ones on furniture repair and refinishing. After all, the same materials and techniques used by early furniture makers were exactly the same as used in finishing older houses.

Throughout the various styles and interior decorating periods, earlier generations were not always content with just naturally finished woods or plain painted surfaces. They inevitably found ways to add color and extra life to many rooms. Sometimes several different colors were used on the ceiling,

Photography: Thomas Strahan Co.

Traditional, Colonial, floral ribbon designed wallpaper with matching borders is used at base and chair rail mouldings. Identical design was used in fabric for window drapes, chair upholstery and bedspread.

Photography: James Seeman Studios

A heart-and-flower-shaped lattice wallpaper design, inspired by a Pennsylvania Dutch coverlet, provides flair for a restored kitchen. Crewel embroidery pattern at fireplace ceiling is repeated below on mantel.

Photography: Katzenbach and Warren, Inc.

Soft charcoal gray wallpaper, highlighted with peach and lavender flowers, reflects a Victorian look. Matching fabric was used on wicker chaise. Small-patterned border was applied as trim, and on the ceiling.

walls, or decorative elements to highlight individual components. Ornate sculptured borders at the ceiling line were accented with subtle contrasting colors. Walls may have been painted different colors or wainscoted with natural wood below and painted above. Chair rail and plate rail mouldings broke up high wall surfaces and added horizontal lines to short walls.

Hand-blocked wallpaper, for those who could afford the luxury, was applied to the total wall or used as frieze strips along the ceiling line with a painted wall below. Ceilings were outlined with decorative borders or complicated geometric patterns, with design elements cut from the wallpapers and selectively pasted to the ceiling. In some instances Victorian interiors might combine vertically striped wallpaper on the lower wall portion with a band of floral patterns above.

Unfortunately, not many of today's wallpaper manufacturers are producing matched sets of patterns for walls, borders, and wide friezes as used in the Victorian era, but some traditional firms, like A.L. Diament, Philadelphia, still supply museum-quality, hand-blocked scenic wallpapers and a number of border designs.

For those less affluent homeowners, the decorative effects of expensive wallpaper were duplicated by using bright stenciled patterns on walls, ceilings, floor, and furniture. The designs most popular included tulips and other flowers, vines with leaves and berries, and a number of swags and tassels draped on walls around windows and doors. The colors were often exciting and lively, rather than somber geometric patterns.

Much of the early stenciling was done by itinerant artists who found the thin stencil patterns cut into oiled paper, leather, or tin to be a portable and profitable way to make a daily living.

Probably the best known artist was Moses Eaton, Jr., who stenciled his way through New England before settling in Dublin, New Hampshire. Fortunately, his original stencil kit, with eight brushes and 78 patterns was found and turned over to the Society for the Preservation of New England Antiquities. By arrangement with the Society, Silver Bridge Reproductions offers a pre-cut kit of some of the Eaton stencil patterns. Other restoration projects, like Old Sturbridge Village and Historic Deerfield in Massachusetts, and the Shelburne Museum in Vermont, offer similar stencil kits.

If you are looking for a real touch of nostalgia in the right period house, you might want to consider installing a "tin ceiling." The embossed metal sheets are available in patterns ranging from the Gay Nineties, with their ornate designs, to the stark, geometrical precision of the Art Deco period. Most metal ceilings come in 24 x 96-inch sheets and are nailed to furring strips on the ceiling. Most are painted, but some are finished with a clear coating, and at approximately one dollar per square foot plus crating and shipping, the cost is reasonable for truly distinctive period ceilings. Decorative ceiling panels are also available in other materials, and can be adhered to sheetrock or plaster ceilings by the do-it-yourselfer.

Metal Refinishing

It is often the details that make the difference between an average and a highly successful restoration project. One detail you should take advantage of is the amount of quality metalwork usually found in older houses—wall and ceiling lighting fixtures, hinges, knobs, and escutcheon plates on doors, the ornate filigree of wall and floor heater grilles, or the brass mail slot cover and knocker that decorate the front door. Some may be solid metal, others brass or copper or

bronze. You may have to scratch in an inconspicuous place through years of tarnish and layers of paint to identify the metal.

Sometimes the refinishing can be accomplished by removing any paint and buffing the surface with fine steel wool or metal polishing compound. For seriously worn or pitted surfaces, you can have the item replated at an industrial refinishing shop. This is an electrochemical process that bonds a similar or different metal surface to the older

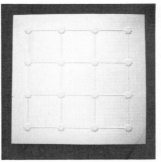

Photography: Ceilings, Walls & More, Inc.

Decorative, three-dimensional ceiling treatments can be applied to any sound surface. Old-fashioned stamped metal ceilings are available in squares or 24 x 96-inch sheets. Plan your design to include decorative borders and ornate ceiling line mouldings. Above, two-foot-square acoustical embossed panels can be applied directly to ceiling or used in drop-ceiling installations. Panels may be painted or left natural.

Photography: Bill Rooney

Older homes often have a wealth of metal work, some solid, some plated, which is well worth cleaning or replating. Brass heating grille, above, was cleaned, polished and coated with clear protective finish.

117

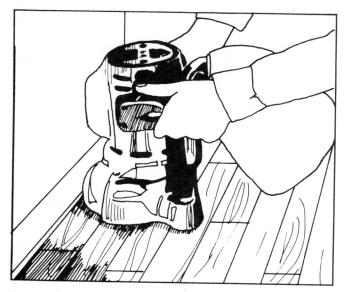

Large, floor model drum sander with coarse and successively finer grades of sandpaper is used on major floor area. However, hand scraping and sanding is necessary to remove old finish in corners.

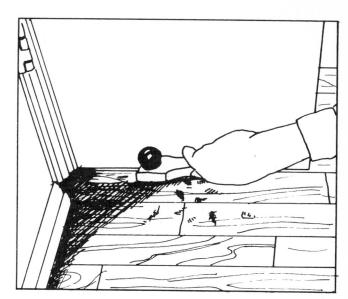

Remove base shoe moulding from wall perimeter and sand with disc edge sander with same grit papers as used on main floor. Obtain sanders and buy various grades of paper needed from your local tool rental.

Remove all sander dust from floor, then vacuum all surfaces including window ledges and baseboards. Open grain woods usually need a neutral filler, applied with a rag or brush for a smooth finish.

A variety of surface and penetrating floor finishes are available. Consult the chart on the facing page to select the best finish for sheen, long wear, and low maintenance that applies to your family activities.

material. Professional platers complete the polishing by buffing on a rouge wheel and applying a baked laquer seal to prevent further tarnishing.

Floor Finishing

By the time you are ready to finish the floors, all other major repairs and finishing projects should be completed. The floors are the last items to be completed in any restoration. You're headed down the home stretch.

The conventional method of floor finishing is to sand off the existing finish and lay down a new protective coating. All nail heads must be driven below the wood surface to prevent tearing the sandpaper. Then, a large drum sander with coarse paper is used to remove the top surface, sanding with the grain whenever possible. A second pass over the floor is made using a medium-grade sandpaper. Usually the shoe moulding along

the room's baseboard is removed and a smaller disc sander is used to strip the floor around the perimeter, door frames, stair treads, and other difficult-to-reach spots.

It will be necessary to use hand scrapers and a small sandpaper block to clean out corners, reach under radiators, and around stair parts. Once the floor is completely sanded, it must be carefully swept and later vacuumed to remove all traces of dust before the finish can be applied.

Should you attempt to do the sanding yourself or should you hire a professional contractor? You can rent the necessary sanders and buy the various grades of sandpaper from a number of rental organizations. Setting the nail heads and completely sanding the floor is a long and tough job. It is dusty, noisy, and monotonous. To be economical, the job should be done all at one time, and the entire house will be a mess for a week or more. By this time in your restoration project, you have logged months of difficult and tiresome work. If your budget can stand the cost, it might be a good time to reward yourself and your family with a vacation and have the floors done by a professional.

Floor sanding has the advantage of leveling out any uneven sections, getting the job done all at one time. The completed project results in a clean, new-looking floor. The disadvantages are loss of patina and character, and dust filtering throughout the house, and, unless done very carefully, the power sanders tend to dig in at some locations leaving unevenness along the sides and corners. If you are working on thin parquet floor tiles, the heavy sanding may create a serious loss of thickness.

An alternative system to sanding is to use a chemical finish remover and strip off the old finish. This has the advantages of eliminating the nail setting step, retaining the old floor, natural patina look, and allowing you to do one room at a time, rather than attacking the entire house at once. The disadvantages are lack of floor leveling, an awful mess and odors, plus the hands and knees labor involved.

If you decide to strip rather than sand, start by working a narrow section around the room edges, first being careful to keep the remover off the finished baseboards. Then work a small section about 18 inches by 4 feet at a time. Use a scraper, steel wool, or burlap rags to completely remove all the old finish. As a final step before refinishing, wipe down the floor area with turpentine or lacquer thinner to neutralize the chemicals that are absorbed by the wood.

Traditional floor finishes include the varnishes and shellacs, but the newer polyurethane products deliver a tougher, longer-lasting surface if you can afford the drying time and don't object to the high-gloss "gym" floor appearance. For a softer, satin look, consider the tung or Swedish penetrating oil finishes. They are easier to apply, and heavy traffic areas can later be touched up without restripping and refinishing. Follow the recommendation of your finishing supplier.

Floor Finish Selector

	Finish Type	Advantages	Disadvantages
Surface Film Types	Shellac	Inexpensive. Easy to apply and touch up by blend-patching.	Not long wearing. Should be waxed. Vulnerable to water. Becomes brittle with age.
	Conventional Varnish	Moderate cost. Longer wearing and more stain-resistant than shellac.	Long drying time. May require filler on oak floors. Surface has gloss. Waxing recommended.
	Quick-Dry Varnish	Fast drying allows room to be put back in service sooner. Easy to touch up by blend-patching. No waxing needed.	Medium wear life. Surface has a gloss.
	Poly-Urethane	Hardest surface of all varnishes. Long-wearing and highly resistant to staining and scarring when properly applied. No waxing.	Can be misapplied. Not compatible with certain stains; plastic film can separate from wood. Can't blend-patch. Surface has a gloss.
Penetrating Types	Penetrating Sealer	Easy to apply and touch up. Doesn't leave glossy reflective film on the surface.	Not long wearing. Waxing is recommended.
	Oil Finish	Final finish has rich lustre and patina. Easy to touch up.	Not long wearing. Long drying time. Will darken with age.

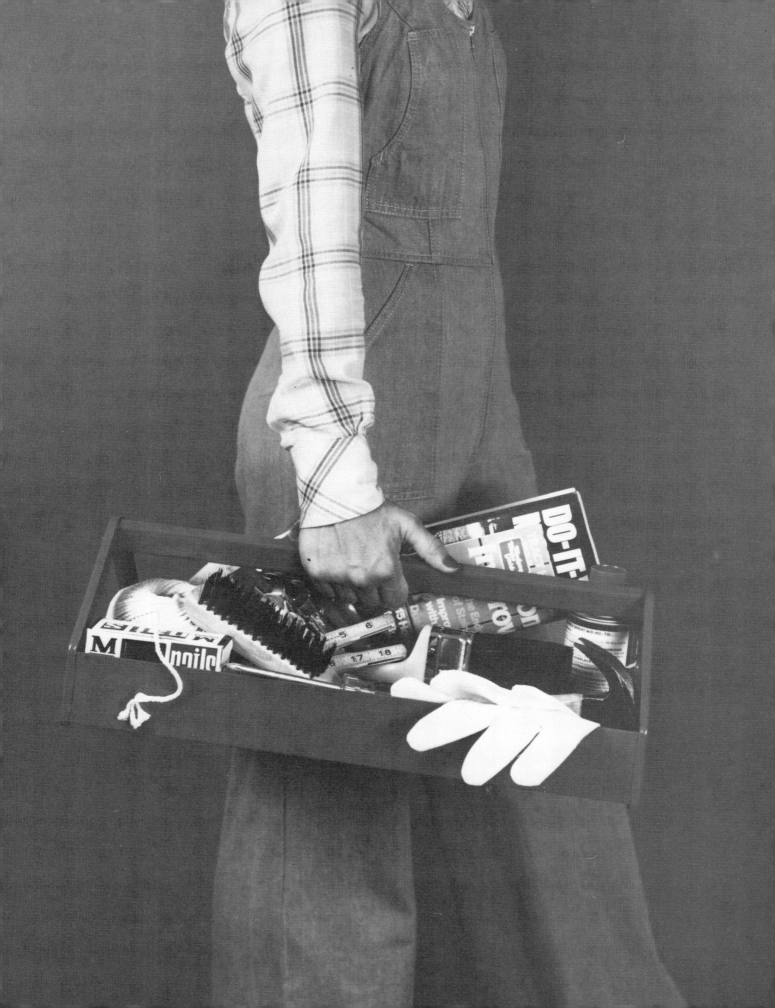

Chapter 8
Practical Restoration

he practical aspects of any restoration project involve the mechanical systems that provide the home with safe, comfortable and efficient living. Although the wiring, plumbing, and climate control systems are usually buried within the structural framework, you can't take them for granted. They represent an integral part of any well-functioning home.

Each system must be carefully inspected, restored in some cases, but more often improved or replaced, and all the work must be done to rather exacting standards. Sometimes, sloppy workmanship creates minor annoyances like water pipes that hammer, slow heating rooms, or awkwardly placed electrical switches. However, more serious problems such as overloaded electrical circuits, bathroom plumbing that backs up, or impure water lines can develop into serious health and safety hazards.

Because of the technical nature of mechanical work and the serious consequences of improperly done installations, rigid inspections are required by all building codes to assure that all systems perform satisfactorily. At best, a bad electrical wiring job may require breaking into a freshly repaired or finished wall to correct the defect. At worst, poor wiring can cause a fire resulting in loss of property or life. Mechanical restoration is not to be taken lightly.

Can the average homeowner restore his own mechanical systems? In almost all cases, the answer is a definite, "NO." While even the greenest amateur with a few tools and a little basic knowledge can rewire a lamp fixture or install a dimmer switch, replace a washer, faucet fixture, or fix a gurgling toilet tank, major work is another story. For several reasons, you should give serious consideration to having all mechanical work done by professionals. They have the experience, manpower, and supply contacts to obtain the proper parts and equipment at the right price. Installing a new furnace or bathtub requires both skill and muscle. Running wiring in ex-isting walls calls for special long drill bits, and plumbing work usually needs a variety of oversize wrenches plus special tools for cutting and threading large pipes.

Even if you have the skills and tools, local building codes may require that the work be completed by a licensed electrician, plumber, or heating contractor. You can usually spend your time more profitably on other portions of a restoration job by allowing the professionals to handle the mechanical aspects alone. If you are working within an extremely limited budget, it is sometimes possible to make arrangements with a contractor, when he bids the job, for you to serve as a "helper" — saving yourself a few dollars by handling the simpler (and sometimes dirtier) parts of the job.

Electrical Systems

Your initial house inspection may provide the starting point for restoring the electrical system. The detailed inspection usually points out all the problem areas of inadequate size capacity on the main electric board, frayed and damaged wiring, and lack of conveniently placed outlets. Once the problems are defined, you then face the task of making corrections and expanding the system to better serve today's increased power needs. In almost all cases, older houses are badly underpowered. An electric clothes washer-dryer combination requires more electricity than was needed for the whole house 20 or 30 years ago.

Since the electric companies are well aware of these rapidly expanding needs, many provide an "adequate wiring survey" free of charge to property owners. This service will help determine your electrical requirements based on the number and type of appliances, size of your family, and the number of circuits needed for various rooms. Now is the time to plan for any additional equipment that you anticipate adding to the house in the future—intercoms, exterior lighting, automatic garage door openers, electric snow melting panels for walks and driveways, and air conditioning systems.

Start your thinking from the outside and work into the house. Is this the time to consider underground wiring for power, telephone, and TV cables? Have them installed during restoration and before the landscaping has been completed. Exterior lighting for security and safety are a welcome addition. If you appreciate the soft welcome of flickering gas lights beside the front walk or entrance, you'll need a plumber, not an electrician, to install the gas lines. With the growing use of outdoor electrical power tools—lawnmowers, hedge clippers, and patio barbecue rotisseries—grounded, three-prong outlets along the foundation and patio make good sense.

Inside, the electrical system breaks down into three parts: the master panel, the branch circuits feeding power to various areas and outlets, and switches and fixtures in each room. The main or master panel is where the power service line is brought into the house. The size of the service line is determined by the amount of power needed to operate the house efficiently.

The minimum requirement for today's house is a three-wire, 240-volt, 100-ampere service. However, if you have more than 3,000 square feet of space, electric heating or central air conditioning, a larger 150- or 200-ampere service will be needed. Older homes generally have a fuse box as a safety device. When too much power is demanded, the fuse blows, shutting off the power before the system becomes overloaded and can cause a fire. Blown fuses must be replaced to restore the system.

Circuit breakers are the modern version of the older fuse box. The circuit breaker automatically flips to an "off" position to prevent an overload on the line. To restore power, merely flip the switch back to the "on" position—much simpler than unscrewing and replacing fuses. If your present fuse box is in good condition, you can leave it in service and add an auxiliary breaker panel to handle new circuit lines. However, it is usually smarter to replace the old fuse box with a larger, more convenient circuit breaker panel. A master switch in the panel allows all power to be shut off at the source.

The master panel has a series of circuits with breakers controlling individual wires to areas within the house. A typical panel may have six or more individual circuits for lights and outlets, several heavy-duty lines for kitchen appliances, and one circuit each for the furnace, water heater, stove, washer, and dryer. It is a good idea to have two or three spare circuits to handle air conditioners or a workshop that might be added later.

In a restoration project, tracing existing wiring can be a difficult and time-consuming job. If the existing wiring is frayed and in poor condition, it may be less expensive to disconnect it and run all new wires. When specifying wiring, the lower the number, the heavier the wire. New wiring should be number 12 or heavier. Lighter, number 14 wire, may cause

Illustration Source: G.E. Co., Wiring Device Business Dept.

A typical electrical system

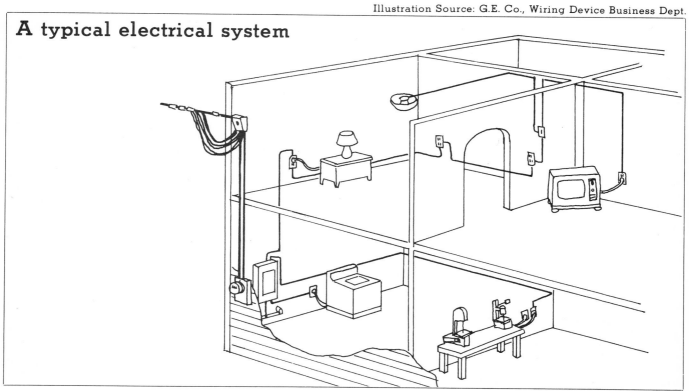

Switch-type circuit breaker

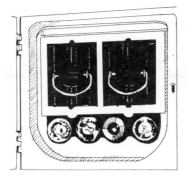

Fuse-type circuit box

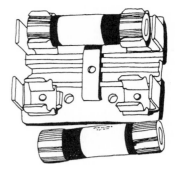

Pull-out unit with 2 cartridge fuses

Time Delay plug fuses

Type S plug fuses

Edison-base plug fuses

Source: Underwriters Lab., Inc.

flickering lights when several lamps and appliances are in use on the same circuit.

Electrical codes specify the number of outlets in each room, but the location is based more on common sense than the minimum requirements. Since most small appliances have cords six feet or less in length, baseboard outlets should be spaced about ten feet apart. Use enough outlets to eliminate the need for extension cords. A series of outlets six feet apart along kitchen countertops is more convenient spacing. Light switches should be placed beside each room door and at the top and bottom of all stairways for maximum safety.

Don't forget to provide extra outlets in the bathroom for electric shavers, hair dryers, and other items. Basement, utility room, and other work areas may have special requirements. Your planning should also include provisions for extra telephone jacks and cable television leads. Other electrical considerations include automatic closet lights, intercoms and door bells, dimmer switches and remote control lighting panels, silent light switches, and no-shock outlets as a safety feature for small children.

Wiring for either wall- or ceiling-mounted light fixtures requires preplanning to determine the exact location. Before you discard

any old gas light fixtures, check with an electrician to determine if the antique fixture can be rewired for electric lighting. Flame-shaped bulbs, although not the most efficient, can add a nostalgic touch when mounted in antique brass fixtures. If you plan to add

Original gas light fixtures can often be wired to accept electrical bulbs. Any restoration project provides the opportunity to install salvaged or new lighting fixtures as long as they are in keeping with the period.

Photography: Sarama

123

Photography: Period Lighting Fixtures

Lighting fixtures should be authentic in design for the restoration period and scaled to fit surroundings. Chandeliers can be as wide as the table and exterior lanterns mounted at eye level or above for best results.

Outdoor lamps can add a traditional look to entryways, as well as provide functional lighting. Left, redwood deck area is illuminated by period lanterns.

heavy chandeliers, a standard electrical box will not support this weight. A special pipe or small beam can be installed to carry the additional weight.

In restoration work, the proper size and placement of electrical fixtures sometimes confuses the homeowner. Richard Scofield, founder of Period Lighting Fixtures, Chester, Connecticut, suggests the following general rules. "When selecting the proper size for a chandelier, do not be afraid of the fixture being too large for a room. More often than not, too small is the problem. The outer most diameter of a chandelier can be as large as the width of a table without interfering with normal traffic. How high or low should it be? The center of the fixture or the drip pans at the base of the candle should be 28 to 35 inches above the table surface depending on total ceiling height and your preference.

"In selecting an outside fixture," said Scofield, "be it a wall-mounted or post lantern, the single most important advice is not to be afraid of the lantern being oversized. You must consider that both your house and the out-of-doors will greatly diminish the size of the fixture. Proper location for wall-mounted fixtures would be eye level or slightly higher. Five to six feet above ground should be the minimum for installation of a post lantern. Any lamp post should be anchored two feet into the ground, preferably in a cement footing."

So that boxes, outlets, and switches can be installed in the correct places, the exact locations should be marked before you begin wiring. Restoration gives you the opportu-

nity to correct and improve your electrical situation. If you have any doubts or questions, consult your local electric utility company.

Plumbing Systems

The residential plumbing system includes the water supply lines, the drainage system, water heater, and various kitchen and bath fixtures. Adequate water pressure is important throughout the entire system. Turn on several faucets on the ground and upper floors to determine if the water flow is adequate. Low pressure is generally caused by either too small a service line from the municipal water main or, more likely, reduced diameter pipes within the house due to

Pipe Identification

Since dissimilar metals corrode when joined together in a plumbing system, use a small magnet and a pen knife to identify your pipes.

1. Copper—when scratched, appears orange in color; a magnet will not stick to copper.
2. Brass—a yellowish-gold color when scratched; magnet will not stick.
3. Lead—gray or silver when scratched; magnet does not stick.
4. Galvanized iron—similar to lead in color but magnet **will** cling to pipe.
5. Cast iron—dull rust color when scratched, coarse rough surface; magnet will stick.

lime or scale deposits building up in old water lines.

Before you or a professional attempt any plumbing repairs, it is necessary to locate the main water shut-off valve. By closing the valve, you can shut off the flow of water to the entire house. Often an old valve that has been undisturbed for years will be rusted tight in the open position. Freeing a frozen valve is a touchy proposition. Excessive pressure on the handle may break the old metal and result in a flooded basement. If the valve will not move with reasonable pressure, soak the works with a penetrating oil or lubricant and let it set for a day. Try again, and if still stuck, apply more oil. If the valve stem will not loosen, then the water must be cut off at the street main and the valve replaced. This is expensive and definitely requires professional help.

Once the water flow is stopped, you can make repairs or replace various parts. The modern house of today uses copper pipes, and some local codes permit plastic pipe for cold water lines or special hot water chlorinated polyvinyl chloride plastic pipes rated for 100 pounds pressure per square inch and for temperatures up to 180 degrees. Older homes may have copper pipes, but more likely brass, lead or galvanized, and cast iron. The basic rule is to use one material only throughout the entire plumbing system. Where several dissimilar materials are used, the joints will corrode from galvanic action.

If you suspect the water supply system leaks, check for signs of rust, white or greenish crusting on the pipes or at the joints. Small leaks in copper lines can be spot soldered. A pin hole leak in a lead pipe can

Many building codes today permit use of newer corrosion-resistant PVC and Polypropylene drainage fittings. They are easy to assemble, light weight, impervious to household chemicals, and are not damaged by hot water or drain cleaners.

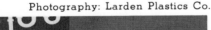
Photography: Larden Plastics Co.

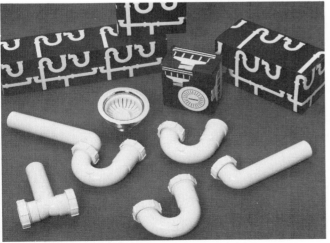

Photography: Genova Inc.

Newer compounds join cast iron pipes to plastic piping with waterproof seal. Material expands as it cures solidly in the joint. When water pressure is shut off, the putty can be used to repair small holes and leaks.

sometimes be sealed by rapping sideways with a hammer close to the hole. The hammer blow often closes over the hole in the soft lead.

More serious leaks in supply pipes can usually be repaired with some of the newer patching compounds. Turn off the water supply and let the pipes dry. You can speed the drying process if you apply heat from a hair dryer, heat lamp, or propane torch if you are careful not to overheat and melt the soft lead. Once dry, clean the area around the leak with a wire brush in an electric drill or with steel wool or emery paper. Clean at least three inches around the problem area. Then apply plastic lead, plastic steel or other metal patching compound, building up a thickness of at least one-eighth inch to plug the leak. Allow the patching material to dry thoroughly before the water is turned back on.

Cast-iron pipe that has cracked or rusted through can be repaired in a similar manner. Once dried and cleaned, large splits or holes are coated with polyester or epoxy resin, wrapped in fiberglass strips, recoated and rewrapped, and a final coating of resin applied to the entire patch. This is allowed to cure for 24 hours before the water is turned back on.

Plumbing noises are not only annoying, but can signal more serious problems. Ticking and groaning in the water supply often occur when hot water is fed into a cold pipe. As the pipe heats up, the metal expands producing the sound. Pipes must be supported throughout the house, but hangers must be flexible enough to allow for slight expansion and contraction as the pipes change temperatures. Gurgling drains may be a sign of improper venting, clogged pipes, or an obstruction in the lines or drainage system. The solution begins with a complete inspection. Check pipes for buildup of scale and deposits, which reduce the inside diameter. Unplug and clean the traps, "J"-shaped plumbing sections beneath the sinks. A snake or auger forced through lines will usually dislodge or break up obstructions. Soil pipes in the drainage system may be ingrown with tree roots, which will have to be removed with a power auger. Overloaded septic tanks should be pumped out and cleaned for efficient performance.

Water hammering should be corrected as soon as possible before serious damage takes place. When water moves rapidly through a pipe when a faucet or washer valve is open and then comes to an abrupt stop when the valve is closed, the backup pressure creates a harsh, hammering sound. Unrelieved, the hammering may break a pipe or plumbing fitting. Air chambers are usually built into a line to cushion the rushing water when a valve is suddenly closed. The line should be drained to restore air to the chambers, or new air chambers installed to solve the hammering condition.

The water heater, since it is the key element in dispensing hot water for clothes and dishwashing as well as personal cleanliness, deserves special consideration. In an older house, the existing water heater is most likely inadequate. It was installed before the popularity of automatic dish and clothes washers. Even if the heater appears to have sufficient tank capacity, if the unit is over ten years old, it may be time for a replacement.

Today, water heaters are available powered by gas, electricity, or the newer oil-fired models. Your choice will depend upon the current system installed, the present and anticipated cost of a particular fuel, and the conversion cost from one system to another. Since all of these factors vary from location to location, check with the service department of your local utilities to obtain current cost information before you decide which of the different models to choose.

You should be aware that the size of tank capacity you choose depends upon the type of fuel, as well as the number and ages in your family, and the number of hot-water-consuming appliances used. For instance, to supply the same family, an electric water heater must be larger than a gas-fired heater. The type of tank lining depends on the hardness or content of the local water supply. In soft water areas, glass, aluminum, ceramic, or copper tanks are recommended. In a hard water area, galvanized heaters can be a better bargain. Consult your local plumber or utility.

The minimum-size electric water heater for the average family is a 66-gallon tank capacity. A household with several small children and a lot of washing may need a larger heater.

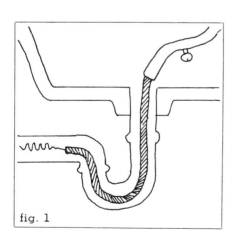

fig. 1

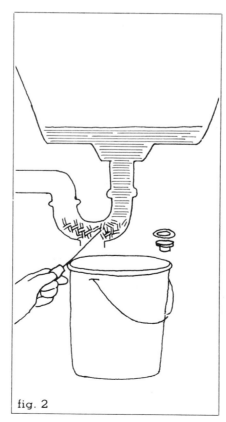

fig. 2

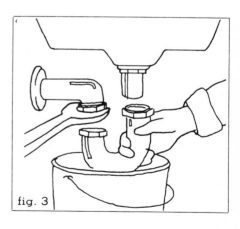

fig. 3

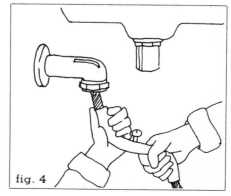

fig. 4

Minor clogged drains can sometimes be freed by using a rubber force cup or "plumber's helper." It's possible to use the plumber's snake without removing the trap (fig. 1). If still blocked, remove cleanout plug (fig. 2). If trap is clean, then blockage is further down the pipe. Cover the chrome trap nut with several layers of tape to protect finish, remove with wrench (fig. 3) and insert plumber's wire snake into line to dislodge any blockage (fig. 4).

Gas Water Heater Size?

Minimal capacity for gas water heaters for various conditions:

Family size	Minimum capacity	With automatic washer
3	30 gal.	30-40 gal.
4	30	40-50
5	30-40	40-50
6	40-50	50-65
7	40-50	65

In addition to tank size, the recovery rate must be taken into account when deciding on a new heater. The rate indicates how fast the water heater can reheat and continue to supply water for showers and washing. High-speed or high-watt electric units can make a 40-gallon tank more efficient than a 50-gallon conventional heater. An acceptable recovery rate is one that can provide at least 30 gallons of hot water an hour. It should be able to heat thirty gallons of 60-degree water to 160 degrees each hour of operation.

Plumbing fixtures for the kitchen and baths may be enameled cast iron or vitreous china. Minor damage on either can sometimes be repaired or resurfaced with the newer epoxy resins. Badly chipped, scratched, or rusted fixtures are usually replaced.

Restoring older bathrooms requires careful consideration. Here, in these private rooms, your personal taste and willingness to compromise authenticity for practicality present some difficult decisions. For some people, a monstrous, claw-footed, cast-iron bathtub represents several hundred pounds of pure nostalgia and must be preserved at any cost. For others, older fixtures are out of date, inefficient, difficult to keep clean and undesirable.

Assuming that the original fixtures are of reasonably good quality, most can be repaired and resurfaced to contribute additional years of service. The inner workings of flush tanks on toilets are simple to repair, and the plumbing industry has taken large steps forward in the past few years by packaging repair parts with explicit installation information and diagrams so that the average homeowner with a few basic tools can handle many repairs. Replacing a washer or regrinding a faucet valve seat are quick, easy, and inexpensive solutions to a leaking faucet.

Second-hand stores and salvage yards offer sets of decorative handles, sinks, and other plumbing fixtures recovered from demolished houses, plus manufacturers today are recreating the old-styled brass bathroom fittings and decorative china parts, both plain and hand-painted. Even the old pull-chain toilets with the tank mounted high overhead on the wall are back in production. While old plumbing fixtures can be repaired or replaced, no one can really fault you if you opt for a more modern bathroom as part of your restoration project.

Heating Systems

The heating system in an older home can be a real adventure. Some are surprisingly efficient even by today's standards. Others can be a disaster. Yours probably falls somewhere in between. It may be a gravity warm-air system or forced air supplied by a blower. It may be circulating hot water or a steam pipe system. The furnace may be the original coal-burning model or one that has been converted to burn gas or oil.

You can do some preliminary checking yourself. Check the boiler name plate to see if the furnace is made of cast iron or steel. If the furnace is wrapped in white asbestos covering, it may provide insulation, but too often on an older model the wrapping may be all that is holding the unit together. Inspect the inside for signs of cracks and corrosion, outside around the base for rust and deterioration. Check the steam or water pipes or the air ducts to determine if valves and baffles operate freely and lines are not rusted or showing signs of leaking.

The only sensible way to determine the efficiency of a heating system is to fire it up and try it. A warm-air heater should become effective within 10 or 15 minutes, a hot-water or steam system within half an hour. If you have a hot-air system, it should operate quietly without noisy rushing air. Check the temperature in each room and see if your heating system operates uniformly throughout the house. Slow response in some areas, or dirt stains around the room vents, could be nothing more than dirty filters at the furnace. This is easily corrected, but if new filters won't solve the problem, you may have more serious and expensive trouble.

In a hot water or steam system, radiators are needed in each room. Heat should spread evenly and the topmost rooms should be as comfortable as those on the first floor. Hissing radiators, and those slow to heat up, may be caused by worn air vent valves. These are easy to replace. If the problem is more serious, then you probably have a boiler that is undersized, damaged, or just plain old.

After your initial inspection, check around the furnace area where a service or repair card is usually posted. Take the name and address of the heating dealer who has serviced the system and give him a phone call. Ask about the type and age of the system, what

Photography: Period Lighting Inc.

Open fireplaces sacrifice heating efficiency for historical authenticity. Note the fieldstone fireplace, slate hearth with collection of antique cooking utensils, and copper wall sconce with flame-shaped electrical bulbs.

repairs have been made, how efficiently it operates and an honest appraisal as to how long the system will last. Most dealers will supply pretty straight answers.

Once you have a good idea of the efficiency and operating costs of your present heating plant, you are in a position to make some decisions. If you are fortunate, your furnace may have a lot of good years left. If not, some coal-burning furnaces can be converted to burn gas or oil. However, the experts say you may be unwise to attempt converting a unit that is more than 15 or 20 years old. Be sure to weigh the entire cost of conversion before you make the move. For instance, to the cost of adding a new oil-burning furnace and the monthly operating bills, you must include the cost of buying and installing a new oil tank.

If your pipes and radiators or air ducts are in good shape, the furnace replacement may be the only cost you face. Count yourself lucky. The price of a new furnace is considerably less than the expense of replacing an entire heating system.

With hot water or steam heat, you still face the question of how to handle the old radiators in each room. To some, these cast-iron dinosaurs are not the most attractive objects, and they hide them by recessing them into walls or

shielding them with radiator covers. Sometimes the radiators are removed and replaced with newer baseboard type of radiant heaters.

Yet many people consider the bulky appearance and decorative details cast into the surface as a charming part of any restoration. Cleaning up the looks of an old radiator usually involves removing rust or layers of accumulated paint. Both rust and multilayers of paint reduce the heat transfer efficiency of these old-style radiators.

To restore the looks of old radiators, everyone who has been through the process agrees that the units should be disconnected before you start the cleaning up job. Once disconnected, you can easily attack all parts for cleaning and repainting. Rust and accumulated paint are stripped with paste remover, commercial dip tanks, wire brushes or wire roto-strippers in a power drill, or sandblasting. Commercial dipping has the advantage of removing part of the scale and rust on the inside as well as the exterior. If you use a mechanical stripping process on the outside, consider making up a solution of baking soda in hot water and flushing out the inside of the radiator. Then follow this process with a rinse of clean water.

Once stripped, some recommend leaving the radiator uncoated for best heating efficiency. Others have used ordinary wall paint to match or contrast with other surfaces in the room. Most, however, repaint the radiator with the traditional aluminum or bronze powder paints with metallic pigments. The use of either spray cans or a paint spraying outfit will save a lot of time and provide a professional-looking job.

Fireplaces are considered by some restorers as part of the home's heating system, but, frankly, an open fireplace is the least efficient method of heating a room. In most cases, you will lose more heat up the chimney by burning wood in an open hearth than you gain. However, the extra warmth and charm a crackling fire adds to any room is well worth the slight heat loss.

Reopening a bricked-over fireplace, or repairing a present one to bring it up to smoke-free operating condition is a good investment. But in most cases, this is not a job for the amateur. Fireplace construction follows a strict formula of height, width, and depth of the firebox, damper size, and flue opening. Special fire brick must be used to line the box and flue, and heat-resistant mortar is required by building codes. Any repairs or modification of a fireplace should be handled by a qualified expert.

Stains or soot on brick and stonework around a fireplace can sometimes be removed by spraying with a standard oven cleaner and scrubbing with a wire or stiff bristle brush. Stubborn stains may require a half-and-half solution of muriatic acid and water. This is a harsh solution so wear gloves and eye goggles for protection.

You can greatly increase the efficiency of an open hearth fireplace by installing a metal firebox unit into the present opening. These prefabricated units push warm air into the room while limiting the amount of heat that escapes up the flue. Some models use a small

Above, two freestanding cast iron stoves from Vermont Castings Inc. show solid construction features. Above left, Mohawk Tempwood stove and Hearth Mate stove, right, are designed to fit into existing fireplace openings. For safety, chimney and stove should be professionally inspected before operating.

fan to circulate heat, while others extend onto the hearth so that the metal firebox radiates warmth as it heats up.

An alternate suggestion used by some restorers is the installation of a freestanding metal stove, perhaps before the fireplace, so that the stove pipe can be run through the existing chimney. A variety of styles, colors and materials are available, but the most efficient are solid cast-iron models, which absorb and retain heat longer than lighter gauge materials. Solid cast-iron and the heaviest-gauge stove pipes are the best buys for a permanent and safe installation.

All wood-burning fireplace and stove systems should be checked out by a local fire marshall or home heating expert. Fireplaces, chimneys, and heating systems are the prime causes of fires in older homes. The experts should give you a top-to-bottom inspection that covers all interior and exterior parts of the heating system.

You may find that the chimney flues are overdue for a thorough cleaning. Over the years, ash, smoke, and soot from burning wood condenses and collects inside the cooler upper portion of the chimney lining. Soot and a thick layer of creosote-like material build up in the flue and once ignited,

A cutaway of a more efficient fireplace, below, shows a Heatilator model which draws room air from lower right into firebox. There it is heated and circulated via fans back into the room. Glass doors, when added across the hearth, prevent warm air from escaping into the chimney.

can burst into a roaring and dangerous chimney fire.

Chimney cleaning can be a do-it-yourself project. You can rent or buy various weighted metal wire brushes to fit your flue size and, working from the rooftop, lower and raise the brushes until the accumulated soot and creosote have been scraped from the flue lining. It is a tough, dirty job as soot billows out the chimney everytime you raise the brush. At the fireplace hearth, unless you have carefully sealed the opening, your room will be flooded with a fine cloud of black soot.

You can clean your own chimney, but a professional chimney sweep can do the job far faster and better. Within an hour, he will spread protective drop cloths over the hearth and start up a powerful 30-gallon vacuum cleaner with a large hose placed into the fireplace opening. He then sweeps the chimney with brushes from both the top and bottom, plus cleans and inspects the fire brick, damper, and smoke shelf. The suction from his powerful vacuum collects the extremely fine soot particles before they have the chance to spread through the room.

To retard the buildup of soot and creosote in the fireplace and chimney flue, pay attention to the type of fuel you burn. Softwood species, such as fir, pine, and spruce contain a large amount of resin. They burn faster with less heat and more residue than hardwoods such as oak, beech, birch, or maple. The hardwoods are more difficult to ignite, but burn slower, hotter, and cleaner. If at all possible, burn dry wood rather than green material. The added moisture in unseasoned fireplace fuel generates more smoke and soot, which is collected on the chimney lining.

Maintaining a Comfortable House

"Energy Efficiency" is the popular phrase today, and conserving the energy needed to heat or cool a home is a laudable goal. But those measures that make economic sense in a newer house may be either unnecessary or actually detrimental in an older house. For instance, blown insulation or foam insulation applied inside the walls of an old frame house can cause paint peeling and interior rotting. Without a moisture barrier, water vapor within the house from washing and cooking collects within the walls, and when cool, will condense into water droplets making the insulation soggy. This moisture within the walls causes paint to peel from the siding and will eventually rot out wood members.

Before you start any extensive insulation projects, installation of air conditioning, or ordering storm windows, stop and analyze just what you have to work with. Generations

Photography: Bill Rooney

Professional top-hatted chimney sweep operates from roof with wire brushes. Below, large canvas dropcloth on hearth, and powerful commercial vacuum tank with large diameter hose collect chimney soot.

ago, when your house was first constructed, builders and homeowners planned for reasonable heating and cooling methods without the benefit of modern science and its proliferation of gadgets.

If you look closely at your present landscaping or at historical pictures of your house, you may notice that evergreen trees were planted on the north and east sides, while deciduous or leaf-bearing trees were on the south and west exposures. During the winter, the evergreens protected the house from the harsh cold of winds from the north and east, while the leafless trees allowed the warming sun to enter the south and western windows. In the summer, the same trees, then in full bloom, shaded the southern and western exposure from the hot rays of the sun.

Shutters, blinds, window shades and drapes as well as awnings all played a part in controlling the environment of early homes. In the summer, the house was opened up each morning to collect the cool night air. As the day began to heat up, shutters, window shades, and awnings protected the sunny side of the house. In winter, the situation was reversed. Shutters and drapes were closed to prevent loss of heat on the cold side of the house, while everything on the sunny side was opened to allow the sun's warmth to stream in.

Wide roof overhangs, double-hung windows, high ceilings, and old-fashioned ceiling fans, broad porches, and even the fireplace damper were all climate-control tools. The wide overhang and wraparound porches offered protection from wind and sun, plus the porch became the most comfortable sleeping spot on a warm summer's night. Double-hung windows could be opened from the bottom, top, or partially opened at both ends for cross ventilation between rooms. High ceilings were definitely cooler than lower-ceilinged rooms, and when coupled with a ceiling fan, provided year-round comfort.

The sudden resurgence in popularity of the wide-bladed, slowly revolving ceiling fan is both nostalgic and practical. They consume far less power than an air conditioner—only as much as a large light bulb. On hot days, the revolving blades set cooling air in motion. During the winter, warm air rises in the room and collects near the ceiling. The ceiling fan can recirculate the hot air back to the floor level, evening out the room temperature and lowering the demand on the furnace.

The fireplace damper provides a simple control device. When opened on a warm day, it allows the hot air to rise up the chimney promoting air circulation within the room. The damper, of course, should be closed on cold days to prevent heat from escaping.

Once you understand how and why an old house was constructed, you begin to appreciate just how efficient it can be. This is not to say that an older house cannot be made more comfortable and efficient by today's standards as well.

Insulation, or more properly energy conservation, is still a worthwhile addition to any house. Energy savings are a matter of both physical improvements and economical living habits. Simple procedures such as shutting windows and doors, setting thermostats at low levels, and having your furnace and air conditioners serviced regularly are all common-sense steps.

For the best return on energy-saving expenditures, start with the simple repairs. Up to 20 percent of the heat loss in the winter comes from leakage of cold air. Caulking all joints around windows and doors, around the foundation and chimneys, and any gaps in the siding or trim boards where air may leak through are basic first steps. Weatherstripping all windows and doors, including the garage door, will pay big dividends. Caulk-

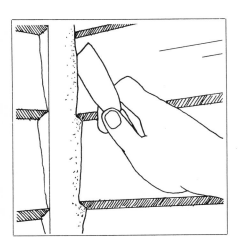

Cracks and openings around windows and doors indicate that it's time to replace caulking. Remove old material with putty knife and clean joints. Caulking cartridges are made to use with handy gun. Squeeze a continuous bead along cracks to seal out cold drafts.

Caulking is also available in rope or cord form. Use it in joints no larger than the thickness of a pencil. Force the caulking into the gaps with your finger or putty knife. Extra wide cracks should be plugged with wood shims or oakum, then caulked.

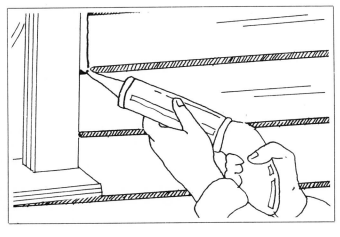

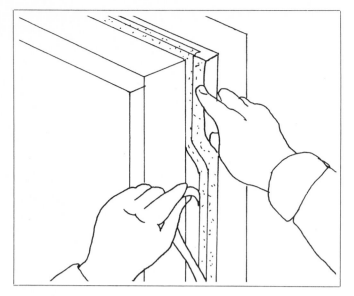

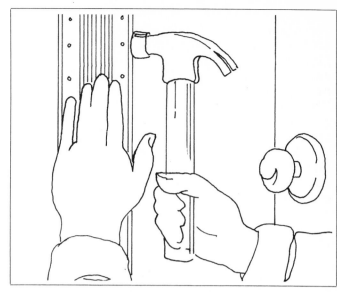

Weatherstripping a door can be done with little difficulty. Adhesive-backed foam is easy to install and is invisible once applied to the door. Stick the foam to the inside of the door jamb and press home.

Another method uses durable metal strips cut to the desired length and tacked in place with screws or nails. Tack one end in place first, then work toward the other end. Avoid bending or damaging the strip.

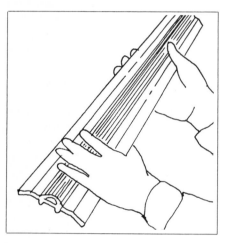

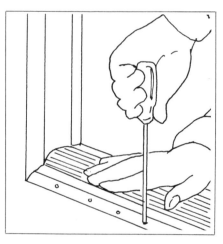

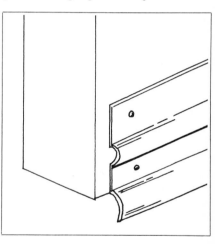

You can reduce energy-wasting drafts at the bottom of exterior doors by replacing worn wooden thresholds. Rust-proof aluminum threshold has vinyl insert for a better weather seal.

Position strip to floor at the threshold directly below door when it's closed and attach to the floor with wood screws. Caulk at ends and along side for tight, wind-proof threshold seal.

As an alternative, attach metal sweeps directly to the exterior door. A rubber flap mounted in an aluminum channel butts snugly against the threshold when the door is closed tightly.

ing is inexpensive and easy to apply with tubes and a caulking gun. Use quality acrylic or butyl caulking for a long-lasting permanent seal. A number of manufacturers today produce caulking in a range of colors to blend with exterior siding colors.

If you are replacing windows during the restoration, investigate the cost-saving potential from use of twin or double-glazed units. These insulated windows have two parallel panes of glass with a sealed air space in between. Windows are produced of aluminum or steel sash, but the traditional wood sash looks more comfortable in a restoration project, and the added insulation value of wood will both conserve energy and reduce

the possibility of condensation compared to metal frames.

Unfortunately, wood storm windows are no longer produced, and some families are reluctant to apply aluminum storm windows on a period-styled home. A local millwork house can produce custom wood storm windows to your sizes, but the cost is usually prohibitive. If shiny aluminum storm windows don't fit your restoration plans, seek out several of the quality manufacturers who produce windows with baked-on colors. These are usually available in white, black, or brown, plus several other colors depending on the individual company. Usually one of the colored storm windows will match or at least harmonize with your exterior color scheme.

Once you have caulked all open joints and considered twin-glazed windows and the addition of storm windows and doors, you should give a serious look at applying insulation where necessary. Since approximately 25 percent of the heat loss in an older house may be through the roof, insulating the attic space is the obvious place to start.

Although it may sound like a contradiction, your local electric or gas utility company can be a big help in answering insulation questions. They are in the business of selling you energy, but today they are just as interested in helping you conserve energy. Most have extensive literature for the do-it-yourself insulator, and many have promotional rebates to save money, or offer free house inspections and recommended insulation procedures. Take advantage of their programs. The following information will also help you answer some insulation questions.

The popular types of insulation include blanket insulation, insulating batts, loose fill insulation, and air blown cellulose fiber insulation. Blankets come in rolls, batts in 4- or 8-foot-long sections. Both are available to fit between 16- or 24-inch on-center ceiling joists and may have a vapor barrier on one side. The loose fill and cellulose fiber are granular in form and come in large bags.

You probably already have the necessary tools for insulating an attic space—a tape measure to figure the square footage to be covered and to measure blanket or batt lengths, a sharp knife, serrated bread knife or hedge shears to cut the insulation. Since the insulation material can cause skin irritation, wear a pair of work gloves and long sleeves. If the attic is without illumination, you will need a portable light and extension cord. A rake or long pole is helpful to push the insulation back under the eaves.

Where the attic is floored with boards, some will have to be removed to allow access. If the joists are uncovered, you will need several 2 x 12-inch planks or sheets of plywood to lay across the joist to walk on. You cannot step in the space between the joist or you will break through the ceiling below.

If there is no insulation in the attic floor, you should use blanket or batts with a vapor barrier, placing the barrier down toward the warm ceiling. Where insulation is already in place, you can add more for greater efficiency, but here, use material without a vapor barrier. Start by installing the insulation under the eaves, but do not butt it tightly against the eaves or cover eave vents. You must allow some room for air circulation at the eave line.

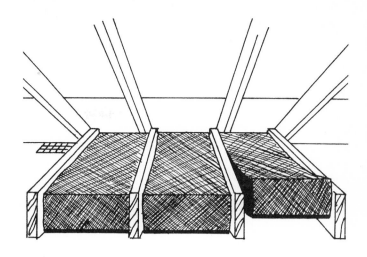

Popular fiberglass roll insulation, cut to length with a serrated bread knife or hedge shears, is lightly pressed into place between the attic floor joist. Vapor barrier is placed down toward the warm or floor side of attic.

Continue inserting the insulation between the joist, but do not cover recessed lighting fixtures, furnace air intakes, or motors that protrude into the attic. Leave at least a 3-inch space around these heat-producing elements to avoid burning the insulation.

Loose fill and air blown insulation should follow the same basic procedure. Smooth out the granular insulation with your rake to the proper depth and build up a cardboard shield to keep the fill at least three inches from any heat-producing elements.

If your house has an unheated basement or crawl space, you should consider using blanket insulation with a vapor barrier. Place the insulation up between the floor joist against the floor underside with the barrier toward the floor above. Either staple the blanket in place, or support between the joist with string or wire mesh to hold in place.

Two final notes:
1. Although information on restoring mechanical systems has been consolidated into this final chapter, you should realize that planning and execution is performed early in the restoration project.
2. Don't try to save money on mechanical systems. Since these are important and possibly expensive projects, it is vital that they be done accurately, safely and conform to strict building code requirements. Professional help and quality building materials are less expensive in the long run than the added cost of undoing and redoing a bad job. Do it right the first time, and you'll have a new "old" home that you can be proud of and will want to display to your close friends.

GLOSSARY

Air-dried lumber. Lumber that has been piled in yards or sheds for any length of time. For the United States as a whole, the minimum moisture content of thoroughly air-dried lumber is 12 to 15 percent and the average is somewhat higher. In the South, air-dried lumber may be no lower than 19 percent.

Alligatoring. Coarse checking pattern characterized by a slipping of the new paint coating over the old coating to the extent that the old coating can be seen through the fissures.

Apron. The flat member of the inside trim of a window placed against the wall immediately beneath the stool.

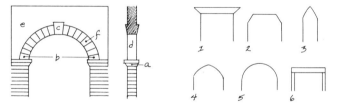

Arch. Opening in a masonry wall. *Parts of the arch:* Impost (a); spring course (b); keystone (c); intrados (d); spandrel (e); extrados (f). *Types of arches:* Flat (Dutch) (1); Segmental (2); Gothic (3); Tudor (4); Round (5); Trabeated (6).

Astragal. A half round moulding; moulding strip covering the junction of a pair of doors or casement windows. See *DOOR*.

Attic. A low story above the main cornice of a classical building.

Attic ventilators. In houses, screen openings provided to ventilate an attic space. They are located in the soffit area as inlet ventilators and in the gable end or along the ridge as outlet ventilators. They can also consist of power-driven fans used as an exhaust system. See *LOUVER*.

Backfill. The replacement of excavated earth into a trench around and against a basement foundation.

Balloon framing. A method of timber-frame construction in which studs run from sill to eaves and the horizontal members are nailed to them.

Balusters. Usually small vertical members in a railing used between a top rail and the stair treads or a bottom rail.

Balustrade. A railing made up of balusters, top rail, and sometimes bottom rail, used on the edge of stairs, balconies, and porches.

Band, band course, bandmould, belt. Flat trim running horizontally in the wall to denote a division in the wall plane or change in level.

Bargeboard, vergeboard. The vertical face board following the roof edge of a gable, often decorated by carving, sometimes called jigsaw woodwork.

Base or baseboard. A board placed against the wall around a room next to the floor to finish properly between floor and plaster.

Base moulding. Moulding used to trim the upper edge of interior baseboard.

Base shoe. Moulding used next to the floor on interior baseboard. Sometimes called a carpet strip.

Batten. Narrow strips of wood used to cover joints or as decorative vertical members over plywood or wide boards.

Bay window. Any window space projecting outward from the walls of a building, either square or polygonal in plan.

Bead, stop bead, bead moulding. A wood strip with round moulded edge against which a window slides or door closes; a cylindral moulding resembling a string of beads.

Beam. A structural member transversely supporting a load.

Bearing partition. A partition that supports any vertical load in addition to its own weight.

Bearing wall. A wall that supports any vertical load in addition to its own weight.

Blind-nailing. Nailing in such a way that the nailheads are not visible on the face of the work—usually at the tongue of matched boards.

Board & Batten. Vertical siding composed of boards butted to one another with a narrow wood member nailed over the butt joint.

Brace. An inclined piece of framing lumber applied to wall or floor to stiffen the structure. Often used on walls as temporary bracing until framing has been completed.

Bracket. A supporting member, similar to a brace, for a projection (floor, shelf, balcony, cornice) often in an "L" shape or triangular truss shape depending on style. "Stop bracket": the large bracket at the end of a row; "bracket shield": the decorative plate at the base of a bracket.

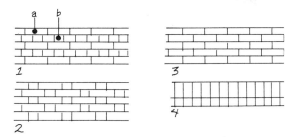

Brick bonds. Common methods of laying brick. *Types:* English (1); Flemish (2); running (3); heading (4). A "stretcher" (a), has its long axis in the plane of the wall; a "header" (b), has its axis normal to the wall plane and bonds with brick behind the outermost course.

Brick veneer. A facing of brick laid against and fastened to sheathing of a frame wall or tile wall construction.

Bridging. Small wood or metal members that are inserted in a diagonal position between the floor joists at midspan to act both as tension and compression members for the purpose of bracing the joists and spreading the action of loads.

Brownstone. Reddish-brown sandstone used to face town- and rowhouses.

Built-up roof. A roofing composed of three to five layers of asphalt felt laminated with coal tar, pitch, or asphalt. The top is finished with crushed slag or gravel. Generally used on flat or low-pitched roofs.

Bullnose. Convex rounding of a horizontal member as the edge of a stair tread. See *STAIR.*

Butt joint. The junction where the ends of two timbers or other members meet in a square-cut joint.

Capital. Top member of a column.

Casement frames and sash. Frames of wood or metal enclosing part or all of the sash, which may be opened by means of hinges affixed to the vertical edges.

Casing. Moulding of various widths and thicknesses used to trim door and window openings at the jambs.

Cement, Keene's. A white finish plaster that produces an extremely durable wall. Because of its density, it excels for use in bathrooms and kitchens and is also used extensively for the finish coat in auditoriums, public buildings, and other places where walls may be subjected to unusually hard wear or abuse.

Centerpiece. A plaster rosette for the center of a ceiling.

Chair rail, dado rail. A strip on wood or plaster wall set as protection against damage from chair backs.

Checking. Fissures that appear with age in many exterior paint coatings, at first superficial, but which in time may penetrate entirely through the coating.

Chimney breast. Section of wall projected to give space for chimney behind.

Chimney piece. The ensemble of architectural treatment around and over a fireplace.

Clear. Milled wood without knots.

Collar beam. Nominal 1- or 2-inch-thick members connecting opposite roof rafters. They serve to stiffen the roof structure.

Column. A perpendicular supporting member, circular or rectangular in section, usually consisting of a base, shaft, and capital.

Combination doors or windows. Combination doors or windows used over regular openings. They provide winter insulation and summer protection and often have self-storing or removable glass and screen inserts. This eliminates the need for handling a different unit each season.

Condensation. In a building: Beads or drops of water (and frequently frost in extremely cold weather) that accumulate on the inside of the exterior covering of a building when warm, moisture-laden air from the interior reaches a point where the temperature no longer permits the air to sustain the moisture it holds. Use of louvers or attic ventilators will reduce moisture condensation in attics. A vapor barrier under the gypsum lath or dry wall on exposed walls will reduce condensation in them.

Construction dry-wall. A type of construction in which the interior wall finish is applied in a dry condition, generally in the form of sheet materials or wood paneling, as contrasted to plaster.

Construction, frame. A type of construction in which the structural parts are wood or depend upon a wood frame for support. In codes, if masonry veneer is applied to the exterior walls, the classification of this type of construction is usually unchanged.

Corbel. A bracket form produced by extending successive courses of masonry beyond the wall surface.

Corner boards. Used as trim for the external corners of a house or other frame structure against which the ends of the siding are finished.

Corner braces. Diagonal braces at the corners of frame structure to stiffen and strengthen the wall.

Cornice. Overhang of a pitched roof at the eave line, usually consisting of a facia board, a soffit for a closed cornice, and appropriate mouldings.

Cove moulding. A moulding with a concave face used as trim or to finish interior corners.

Crawl space. A shallow space below the living quarters of a basementless house, normally enclosed by the foundation wall.

Cresting. Decorative iron tracery or jigsaw work placed at the ridge of a roof.

Cripple stud. A stud that does not extend full height. See *PENNY.*

Cross-bridging. Diagonal bracing between adjacent floor joists, placed near the center of the joist span to prevent joists from twisting.

Dado. A rectangular groove across the width of a board or plank. In interior decoration, a special type of wall treatment.

Decay. Disintegration of wood or other substance through the action of fungi.

Dewpoint. Temperature at which a vapor begins to deposit as a liquid. Applies especially to water in the atmosphere.

Dimension. See *LUMBER DIMENSION*.

Direct nailing. To nail perpendicular to the initial surface or to the junction of the pieces joined. Also termed *face nailing*.

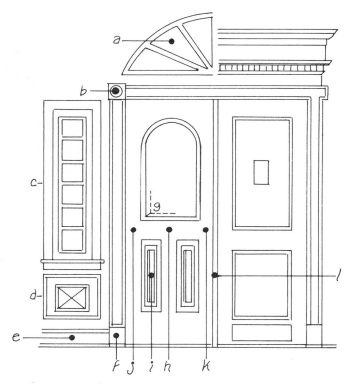

Doors. *Elements:* fanlight (a); bullseye (b); sidelight (c); apron (d); baseboard and shoe (e); stopblock (f); bevelled or etched glass (g); rail (h); panel (i); hinge stile (j); shutting stile (k); astragal (l).

Door jamb, interior. The surrounding case into which and out of which a door closes and opens. It consists of two upright pieces, called side jambs, and a horizontal head jamb.

Dormer. An opening in a sloping roof, the framing of which projects out to form a vertical wall suitable for windows or other openings.

Dormer window. A window placed vertically in a sloping roof and with a roof of its own.

Downspout. A pipe, usually of metal, for carrying rainwater from roof gutters.

Drip. (a) A member of a cornice or other horizontal exterior-finish course that has a projection beyond the other parts for throwing off water. (b) A groove in the underside of a sill or drip cap to cause water to drop off on the outer edge instead of drawing back and running down the face of the building.

Drip cap. A moulding placed on the exterior top side of a door or window frame to cause water to drip beyond the outside of the frame.

Dry-wall. Interior covering material, such as gypsum board or plywood, which is applied in large sheets or panels.

Ducts. In a house, usually round or rectangular metal pipes for distributing warm air from the heating plant to rooms, or air from a conditioning device or as cold air returns. Ducts are also made of asbestos and composition materials.

Eaves. The margin or lower part of a roof projecting over the wall.

Elevation. The external faces of a building; also a drawing made in projection on a vertical plane to show any one face of a building.

Facia or fascia. A flat board, band, or face, used sometimes by itself but usually in combination with mouldings, often located at the outer face of the cornice.

Fan light. See DOOR.

Finial. A formal ornament at the top of a canopy, gable, pinnacle, etc.

Fire stop. A solid, tight closure of a concealed space, placed to prevent the spread of fire and smoke through such a space. In a frame wall, this will usually consist of 2 x 4 cross blocking between studs.

Flashing. Sheet metal or other material used in roof and wall construction to protect a building from water seepage.

Flat paint. An interior paint that contains a high proportion of pigment and dries to a flat or lusterless finish.

Flue. The space or passage in a chimney through which smoke, gas, or fumes ascend. Each passage is called a flue, which together with any others and the surrounding masonry make up the chimney.

Flue lining. Fire clay or terra-cotta pipe, round or square, usually made in all ordinary flue sizes and in 2-foot lengths, used for the inner lining of chimneys with the brick or masonry work around the outside. Flue lining in chimney runs from about a foot below the flue connection to the top of the chimney.

Footing. A masonry section, usually concrete, in a rectangular form wider than the bottom of the foundation wall or pier it supports.

Formwork. The temporary form that "wet" concrete is poured into; constructed of braced timber or metal.

Foundation. The supporting portion of a structure below the first-floor construction, or below grade, including the footings.

Frame construction. A structure whose weight is carried by the framework instead of by load-carrying walls.

Framing, balloon. A system of framing a building in which all vertical structural elements of the bearing walls and partitions consist of single pieces extending from the top of the foundation sill plate to the roofplate and to which all floor joists are fastened.

Framing, platform. A system of framing a building in which floor joists of each story rest on top plates of the story below or on the foundation sill for the first story, and the bearing walls and partitions rest on the subfloor of each story.

French window. A long window reaching to floor level and opening in two leaves like a pair of doors.

Fretwork. A geometrically meandering strap pattern.

Frieze. In house construction, a horizontal member connecting the top of the siding with the soffit of the cornice.

Frostline. The depth of frost penetration in soil. This depth varies in different parts of the country. Footings should be placed below this depth to prevent movement.

Fungi, wood. Microscopic plants that live in damp wood and cause mold, stain, and decay.

Fungicide. A chemical that is poisonous to fungi.

Furring. Strips of wood or metal applied to a wall or other surface to even it and normally to serve as a fastening base for finish material.

Gable. In house construction, the portion of the roof above the eave line of a double-sloped roof.

Gable end. An end wall having a gable.

Gambrel roof. See *ROOF.*

Gazebo. A small tower or summerhouse with a view, usually in a garden or park but sometimes on the roof of a house.

Girder. A large or principal beam of wood or steel used to support concentrated loads at isolated points along its length.

Gloss enamel. A finishing material made of varnish and sufficient pigments to provide opacity and color, but little or no pigment of low opacity. Such an enamel forms a hard coating with maximum smoothness of surface and a high degree of gloss.

Gloss (paint or enamel). A paint or enamel that contains a relatively low proportion of pigment and dries to a sheen or luster.

Grain. The direction, size arrangement, appearance, or quality of the fibers in wood.

Grain, edge (vertical). Edge-grain lumber has been sawed parallel to the pith of the log and approximately at right angles to the growth rings; i.e., the rings form an angle of 45° or more with the surface of the piece.

Grain, flat. Flat-grain lumber has been sawed parallel to the pitch of the log and approximately tangent to the growth rings, i.e., the rings form an angle of less than 45° with the surface of the piece.

Grain, quartersawn. Another term for edge grain.

Graining. A practice of imitating the grain of woods with paint.

Grout. Mortar made of such consistency (by adding water) that it will just flow into the joints and cavities of the masonry work and fill them solid.

Gusset. A flatwood, plywood, or similar type member used to provide a connection at intersection of wood members. Most commonly used at joints of wood trusses. They are fastened by nails, screws, bolts, or adhesives.

Gutter or eave trough. A shallow channel or conduit of metal or wood set below and along the eaves of a house to catch and carry off rainwater from the roof.

Gypsum plaster. Gypsum formulated to be used with the addition of sand and water for base-coat plaster.

Header. (a) A beam placed perpendicular to joists and to which joists are nailed in framing for chimney, stairway, or other opening. (b) A wood lintel.

Heartwood. The wood extending from the pith to the sapwood, the cells of which no longer participate in the life processes of the tree.

Hip. The external angle formed by the meeting of two sloping sides of a roof.

Hip roof. A roof that rises by inclined planes from all four sides of a building.

Humidifier. A device designed to increase the humidity within a room or a house by means of the discharge of water vapor. They may consist of individual room-size units or larger units attached to the heating plant to condition the entire house.

Insulation board, rigid. A structural building board made of coarse wood or cane fiber in 1/2- or 25/32-inch thicknesses. It can be obtained in various size sheets, in various densities, and several treatments.

Insulation, thermal. Any material high in resistance to heat transmission that, when placed in the walls, ceiling or floors, will reduce the rate of heat flow.

Interior finish. Material used to cover the interior framed areas, or materials of walls and ceilings.

Iron, wrought. Iron that is rolled or hammered into shape, never melted.

Jack post. A hollow metal post with a jack screw in one end so it can be adjusted to the desired height.

Jack rafter. A rafter that spans the distance from the wallplate to a hip, or from a valley to a ridge.

Jamb. The side and head lining of a doorway, window, or other opening.

Joint. The space between the adjacent surfaces of two members or components joined and held together by nails, glue, cement, mortar, or other means.

Joint cement. A powder that is usually mixed with water and used for joint treatment in gypsum-wallboard finish. Often called "spackle".

Joist. One of a series of parallel beams, usually 2 inches in thickness, used to support floor and ceiling loads, and supported in turn by larger beams, girders, or bearing walls.

Kiln-dried lumber. Lumber that has been kiln dried often to a moisture content of 6 to 12 percent. Common varieties of softwood lumber, such as framing lumber, are dried to a somewhat higher moisture content.

Kiosk. A small pavilion, such as a garden shelter.

Knob. A projecting round or oval decorative element simulating the shape of a functional knob.

Knot. In lumber, the portion of a branch or limb of a tree that appears on the edge or face of the piece.

Landing. A platform between flights of stairs or at the termination of a flight of stairs.

Lath. A building material of wood, metal, gypsum, or insulating board that is fastened to the frame of a building to act as a plaster base.

Leaded lights. Rectangular or diamond-shaped panes of glass set in lead cames to form a window.

Lean-to. A subordinate building, the ridge of its single-slope roof supported by the major structure.

Ledger strip. A strip of lumber nailed along the bottom of the side of a girder on which joists rest.

Lintel. A horizontal structural member that supports the load over an opening such as a door or window.

Lookout. A short wood bracket or cantilever to support an overhang portion of a roof or the like, usually concealed from view.

Louver. An opening with a series of horizontal slats so arranged as to permit ventilation but to exclude rain, sunlight, or vision. See *ATTIC VENTILATORS*.

Lumber. Lumber is the product of the sawmill and planing mill not further manufactured other than by sawing, resawing, and passing lengthwise through a standard planing machine, crosscutting to length, and matching.

Lumber, boards. Yard lumber less than 2 inches thick and 2 or more inches wide.

Lumber, dimension. Yard lumber from 2 inches to, but not including, 5 inches thick and 2 or more inches wide. Includes joists, rafters, studs, plank, and small timbers.

Lumber, dressed size. The dimension of lumber after shrinking from green dimension and after machining to size or pattern.

Lumber, matched. Lumber that is dressed and shaped on one edge in a grooved pattern and on the other in a tongued pattern.

Lumber, shiplap. Lumber that is edge-dressed to make a close rabbeted or lapped joint.

Lumber, timbers. Yard lumber 5 or more inches in least dimension. Includes beams, stringers, posts, caps, sills, girders, and purlins.

Lumber, yard. Lumber of those grades, sizes, and patterns which are generally intended for ordinary construction, such as framework and rough coverage of houses.

Mansard roof. See *ROOF*.

Mantel. The shelf above a fireplace. Also used in referring to the decorative trim around a fireplace opening.

Mantelpiece. The shelf facing embellishment of a fireplace opening.

Masonry. Stone, brick, concrete, hollow-tile, concrete-block, gypsum-block, or other similar building units or materials or a combination of the same, bonded together with mortar to form a wall, pier, buttress, or similar mass.

Mastic. A pasty material used as a cement (as for setting tile) or a protective coating (as for thermal insulation or waterproofing).

Metal lath. Sheets of metal that are slit and drawn out to form openings. Used as a plaster base for walls and ceilings and as reinforcing over other forms of plaster base.

Millwork. Generally all building materials made of finished wood and manufactured in millwork plants and planing mills are included under the term "millwork." It includes such items as inside and outside doors, window and door frames, blinds, porchwork, mantels, panelwork, stairways, mouldings, and interior trim. It normally does not include flooring, ceiling, or siding.

Miter joint. The joint of two pieces at an angle that bisects the joining angle. For example, the miter joint at the side and head casing as a door opening is made at a 45° angle.

Moisture content of wood. Weight of the water contained in the wood, usually expressed as a percentage of the weight of the oven-dry wood.

Moulding. A wood strip having a curved or projecting surface used for decorative purposes.

Mullion. A vertical bar or divider in the frame between windows, doors, or other openings.

Muntin. A small member that divides the glass or openings of sash or doors.

Natural finish. A transparent finish that does not seriously alter the original color or grain of the natural wood. Natural finishes are usually provided by sealers, oils, varnishes, water-repellent preservatives, and other similar materials.

Newel. A post to which the end of a stair railing or balustrade is fastened. Also, *any* post to which a railing or balustrade is fastened.

Nonbearing wall. A wall supporting no load other than its own weight.

Nosing. The projecting edge of a moulding or drip. Usually applied to the projecting moulding on the edge of a stair tread.

O.C., on center. The measurement of spacing for studs, rafters, joists, and the like in a building from the center of one member to the center of the next.

Oriel. A projecting window with its support corbeled or bracketed; a round or slanted bay window.

Overhand. The projection of a member beyond the face below.

Paint. A combination of pigments with thinners or oils to provide decorative and protective coatings.

Panel. In house construction, a thin flat piece of wood, plywood, or similar material, framed by stiles and rails as in a door or fitted into grooves of thicker material with moulded edges for decorative wall treatment.

Paper, building. A general term for papers, felts, and similar sheet materials used in buildings without reference to their properties or uses.

Parapet. A low retaining wall at the edge of a roof, porch or terrace.

Parting stop or strip. A small wood piece used in the side and head jambs of double-hung windows to separate upper and lower sash.

Partition. A wall that subdivides spaces within any story of a building.

Patio. An open court enclosed on three or four sides by elements of a building.

Pedestal. A base for a column, or for a piece of sculpture or the like.

Pediment. The triangular face of a roof gable or an ornamental construction simulating such.

Penny. As applied to nails, it originally indicated the price per hundred. The term now serves as a measure of nail length and is abbreviated by the letter *d*.

Perm. A measure of water vapor movement through a material (grains per square foot per hour per inch of mercury difference in vapor pressure).

Pier. A column of masonry, usually rectangular in horizontal cross section, used to support other structural members.

Pigment. A powdered solid in suitable degree of subdivision for use in paint or enamel.

Pitch. The incline slope of a roof or the ratio of the total rise to the total width of a house, i.e., an 8-foot rise and 24-foot width is a one-third pitch roof. Roof slope is expressed in the inches of rise per foot of run.

Plan. A graphic representation of a building as cut by an arbitrary, horizontal plane, although it may include surrounding objects as seen from above.

Plaster grounds. Strips of wood used as guides or strike-off edges around window and door openings and at base of walls.

Plate. Sill plate: a horizontal member anchored to a masonry wall. Sole plate: bottom horizontal member of a frame wall. Top plate: top horizontal member of a frame wall supporting ceiling joists; rafters, or other members.

Plinth. The base block of a column.

Plough. To cut a lengthwise groove in a board or plank.

Plumb. Exactly perpendicular; vertical.

Ply. A term to denote the number of thicknesses or layers of roofing felt, veneer in plywood, or layers in built-up materials, in any finished piece of material.

Plywood. A piece of wood made of three or more layers of veneer joined with glue, and usually laid with the grain of adjoining plies at right angles. Almost always an odd number of plies are used to provide balanced construction.

Pointing. The final filling and finishing of mortar joints that have been left raw or raked out.

Porch. A covered entrance.

Portico. An entrance porch.

Precast. Concrete which has been cast before placement on the building.

Preservative. Any substance that, for a reasonable length of time, will prevent the action of wood-destroying fungi, borers of various kinds, and similar destructive agents when the wood has been properly coated or impregnated with it.

Primer. The first coat of paint in a paint job that consists of two or more coats; also the paint used for such a first coat.

Putty. A type of cement usually made of whiting and boiled linseed oil, beaten or kneaded to the consistency of dough, and used in sealing glass in sash, filling small holes and crevices in wood, and for similar purposes.

Quarter round. A small moulding that has the cross section of a quarter circle.

Rabbet. A rectangular longitudinal groove cut in the corner edge of a board or plank.

Radiant heating. A method of heating, usually consisting of a forced hot water system with pipes placed in the floor, wall, or ceiling; or with electrically heated panels.

Rafter. One of a series of structural members of a roof designed to support roof loads. The rafters of a flat roof are sometimes called roof joists.

Rafter, hip. A rafter that forms the intersection of an external roof angle.

Rafter, valley. A rafter that forms the intersection of an internal roof angle. The valley rafter is normally made of double 2-inch thick members.

Rail. Cross members of panel doors or of a sash. Also the upper and lower members of a balustrade or staircase extending from one vertical support, such as a post, to another.

Rake. Trim members that run parallel to the roof slope and form the finish between the wall and a gable roof extension.

Reflective insulation. Sheet material with one or both surfaces of comparatively low heat emissivity, such as aluminum foil. When used in building construction the surfaces face air spaces, reducing the radiation across the air space.

Reinforcing. Steel rods or metal fabric placed in concrete slabs, beams, or columns to increase their strength.

Relative humidity. The amount of water vapor in the atmosphere, expressed as a percentage of the maximum quantity that could be present at a given temperature. (The actual amount of water vapor that can be held in space increases with the temperature.)

Resorcinol glue. A glue that is high in both wet and dry strength and resistant to high temperatures. It is used for gluing lumber or assembly joints that must withstand severe service conditions.

Retaining wall. Wall placed at change of level to prevent shifting of earth.

Ridge. The horizontal line at the junction of the top edges of two sloping roof surfaces.

Ridge board. The board placed on edge at the ridge of the roof into which the upper ends of the rafters are fastened.

Rise. In stairs, the vertical height of a step or flight of stairs.

Riser. Each of the vertical boards closing the spaces between the treads of stairways.

Roll roofing. Roofing material, composed of fiber and saturated with asphalt, that is supplied in 36-inch wide rolls with 108 square feet of material. Weights are generally 45 to 90 pounds per roll.

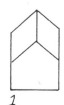 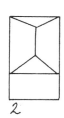 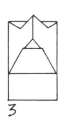 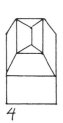

1   2   3   4

Roof, shapes. Gable (1); hipped (2); gambrel (3); mansard (4).

Roof Sheathing. The boards or sheet material fastened to the roof rafters on which the shingle or other roof covering is laid.

Rosette. A conventionalized circular floral motif, usually sculptural.

Rout. The removal of material, by cutting, milling or gouging, to form a groove.

Row house. A house in a row, joined to its neighbors by party walls and covered by the same roof.

Run. In stairs, the net width of a step or the horizontal distance covered by a flight of stairs.

Rustication. Masonry in which the principal face of each stone is rough or highly patterned with a tooled margin.

Saddle. Two sloping surfaces meeting in a horizontal ridge, used between the backside of a chimney, or other vertical surface, and a sloping roof.

Saddle, threshold. A piece which sits under a door bridging flooring materials.

Sand blasting. A method of cleaning or engraving hard surfaces. Very damaging to exterior finish materials.

Sapwood. The outer zone of wood, next to the bark. In the living tree it contains some living cells (the heartwood contains none), as well as dead and dying cells. In most species, it is lighter colored than the heartwood. In all species, it is lacking in decay resistance.

Sash. A single light frame containing one or more lights of glass.

Sash balance. A device, usually operated by a spring or tensioned weatherstripping designed to counterbalance double-hung window sash.

Saturated felt. A felt which is impregnated with tar or asphalt.

Scratch coat. The first coat of plaster, which is scratched to form a bond for the second coat.

Screed. A small strip of wood, usually the thickness of the plaster coat, used as a guide for plastering.

Scribing. Fitting woodwork to an irregular surface. In mouldings, cutting the end of one piece to fit the molded face of the other at an interior angle to replace a miter joint.

Sealer. A finishing material, either clear or pigmented, that is usually applied directly over uncoated wood for the purpose of sealing the surface.

Semigloss paint or enamel. A paint or enamel made with a slight insufficiency of nonvolatile vehicle so that its coating, when dry, has some luster but is not very glossy.

Shake. A thick handsplit shingle, resawed to form two shakes, usually edge-grained.

Sheathing. The structural covering, usually wood boards or plywood, used over studs or rafters of a structure. Structural building board is normally used only as wall sheathing.

Sheet metal work. All components of a house employing sheet metal, such as flashing, gutters, and downspouts.

Shellac. A transparent coating made by dissolving *lac*, a resinous secretion of the lac bug (a scale insect that thrives in tropical countries, especially India), in alcohol.

Shingles. Roof covering of asphalt, asbestos, wood, tile, slate, or other material cut to stock lengths, width, and thicknesses.

Shingles, siding. Various kinds of shingles, such as wood shingles of shakes and nonwood shingles, that are used over sheathing for exterior sidewall covering of a structure.

Shiplap. See *LUMBER, SHIPLAP.*

Shutter. Usually lightweight louvered or flush wood or nonwood frames in the form of doors located at each side of a window. Some are made to close over the window for protection; others are fastened to the wall as a decorative device.

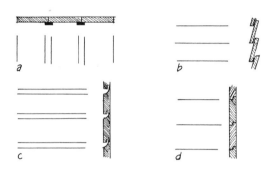

Siding. Boards nailed to framing to provide finish surface to building. *Patterns:* board and batten (a); clapboard (b); drop siding or 'rustic' (c); flush siding (d).

Siding, bevel (lap siding). Wedge-shaped boards used as horizontal siding in a lapped pattern. This siding varies in butt thickness from 1/2 to 3/4 inch and in widths up to 12 inches. Normally used over some type of sheathing.

Siding, Dolly Varden. Beveled wood siding which is rabbeted on the bottom edge.

Siding, drop. Usually 3/4 inch thick and 6 and 8 inches wide with tongued-and-grooved shiplap edges. Often used as siding without sheathing in secondary buildings.

Sill. The lowest member of the frame of a structure, resting on the foundation and supporting the floor joists or the uprights of the wall. The member forming the lower side of an opening, as a door sill, window sill.

Sleeper. Usually, a wood member embedded in concrete, as in a floor, that serves to support and to fasten subfloor or flooring.

Soffit. Usually the underside of an overhanging cornice.

Soil cover (ground cover). A light covering of plastic film, roll roofing, or similar material used over the soil in crawl spaces of buildings to minimize moisture permeation of the area.

Soil stack. A general term for the vertical main of a system of soil, waste, or vent piping.

Sole or sole plate. See *PLATE.*

Solid bridging. A solid member placed between adjacent floor joists near the center of the span to prevent joists from twisting.

Spall. To split off from the surface as in deterioration of stone or concrete.

Span. The distance between structural supports such as walls, columns, piers, beams, girders, and trusses.

Splash block. A small masonry block laid with the top close to the ground surface to receive roof drainage from downspouts and to carry it away from the building.

Square. A unit of measure—100 square feet—usually applied to roofing material. Sidewall coverings are sometimes packed to cover 100 square feet and are sold on that basis.

Stain, shingle. A form of oil paint, very thin in consistency, intended for coloring wood with rough surfaces, such as shingles, without forming a coating of significant thickness or gloss.

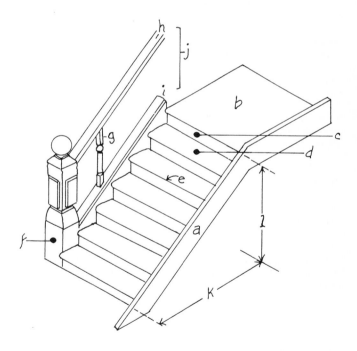

Stair. *Elements:* Carriage, stringer (a); landing (b); riser (c); tread (d); bullnose (e); newel post (f); baluster, 'banister' (g); handrail (h); base (i); balustrade (j); run (k); rise (l).

Stair carriage. Supporting member for stair treads. Usually a 2-inch plank notched to receive the treads; sometimes called a "rough horse."

Stair landing. See *LANDING.*

Stile. An upright framing member in a panel door.

Stool. A flat moulding fitted over the window sill between jambs and contacting the bottom rail of the lower sash.

Storm sash or storm window. An extra window usually placed on the outside of an existing one as additional protection against cold weather.

Story. That part of a building between any floor and the floor or roof next above.

Strike plate. A metal plate mortised into or fastened to the face of a door-frame side jamb to receive the latch or bolt when the door is closed.

Strip flooring. Wood flooring consisting of narrow, matched strips.

String, stringer. A timber or other support for cross members in floors or ceilings. In stairs, the support on which the stair treads rest; also stringboard.

Stucco. Most commonly refers to an outside plaster made with Portland cement as its base.

Stud. One of a series of slender wood or metal vertical structural members placed as supporting elements in walls and partitions. (Plural: Studs or studding.)

Subfloor. Boards or plywood laid on joists over which a finish floor is to be laid.

Suspended ceiling. A ceiling system supported by hanging it from the overhead structural framing.

Template. Pre-cut pattern.

Termites. Insects that superficially resemble ants in size, general appearance, and habit of living in colonies; hence, they are frequently called "white ants." Subterranean termites establish themselves in buildings not by being carried in with lumber, but by entering from ground nests after the building has been constructed. If unmolested, they eat out the woodwork, leaving a shell of sound wood to conceal their activities, and damage may proceed so far as to cause collapse of parts of a structure before discovery. There are about 56 species of termites known in the United States; but the two major ones, classified by the manner in which they attack wood, are ground-inhabiting or subterranean termites (the most common) and dry-wood termites, which are found almost exclusively along the extreme southern border and the Gulf of Mexico in the United States.

Terra cotta. Baked clay used as ornament or exterior surfacing.

Threshold. A strip of wood or metal with beveled edges used over the finish floor and the sill of exterior doors.

Toenailing. To drive a nail at a slant with the initial surface in order to permit it to penetrate into a second member.

Tongue & groove. Boards having a tongue on one edge and a groove on the next for tight joining.

Tread. The horizontal board in a stairway on which the foot is placed.

Trim. The finish material in a building, such as mouldings, applied around openings (window trim, door trim) or at the floor and ceiling of rooms (baseboard, cornice, and other mouldings).

Trimmer. A beam or joist to which a header is nailed in framing for a chimney, stairway, or other opening.

Truss. A frame or jointed structure designed to act as a beam of long span, while each member is usually subjected to longitudinal stress only, either tension or compression.

Turpentine. A volatile oil used as a thinner in paints and as a solvent in varnishes. Chemically, it is a mixture of terpenes.

Turret. A small tower.

Undercoat. A coating applied prior to the finishing or top coats of a paint job. It may be the first of two or the second of three coats. In some usage of the word it may become synonymous with priming coat.

Underlayment. A material placed under finish coverings, such as flooring, or shingles, to provide a smooth, even surface for applying the finish.

Valley. The internal angle formed by the junction of two sloping sides of a roof.

Vapor barrier. Material used to retard the movement of water vapor into walls and prevent condensation in them. Usually considered as having a perm value of less than 1.0. Applied separately over the warm side of exposed walls or as a part of batt or blanket insulation.

Varnish. A thickened preparation of drying oil or drying oil and resin suitable for spreading on surfaces to form continuous, transparent coatings, or for mixing with pigments to make enamels.

Vehicle. The liquid portion of a finishing material; it consists of binder (nonvolatile) and volatile thinners.

Veneer. Thin sheets of wood made by rotary cutting or slicing of a log.

Vent. A pipe or duct which allows flow of air as an inlet or outlet.

Wainscoting (dado). An overlining for interior wall surfaces usually on the lower portion of the wall and topped by a moulding.

Water-repellent preservative. A liquid designed to penetrate into wood and impart water repellency and a moderate preservative protection. It is used for millwork, such as sash and frames, and is usually applied by dipping.

Weatherstrip. Narrow or jamb-width sections of thin metal or other material to prevent infiltration of air and moisture around windows and doors. Compression weather stripping prevents air infiltration, provides tension, and acts as a counterbalance.

Weephole. A hole for drainage in a retaining wall or parapet.

SOURCES

Societies, Groups,
Organizations,
and Government Agencies

Advisory Council on
Historic Preservation
1522 K St., N.W.
Washington, DC 20005

American Assn. for State
and Local History
1400 8th Ave., S.
Nashville, TN 37203

American Institute of Architects
Committee on Historic Resources
1735 New York Ave., N.W.
Washington, DC 20006

American Institute of Planners
1776 Massachusetts Ave., N.W.
Washington, DC 20036

American Society of Planning Officials
Planning Advisory Service
1313 E. 60th St.
Chicago, IL 60637

Brownstone Revival Committee
230 Park Ave.
New York, NY 10017

Commission for Historical
and Architectural Preservation
402 City Hall
Baltimore, MD 21202

Director, National Park Service
U.S. Dept. of the Interior
Washington, DC 20240

Fan District Assn.
P.O. Box 5268
Richmond, VA 23220

Federal Home Loan Bank Board
Urban Reinvestment Task Force
320 1st St., N.W.
Washington, DC 20552

Historic Charleston Foundation
51 Meeting St.
Charleston, SC 29401

Historical Preservation Commission
Old State House
150 Benefit St.
Providence, RI 02903

Historic Richmond Foundation
2407 E. Grace St.
Richmond, VA 23223

Historic Savannah Foundation
119 Habersham St.
Savannah, GA 31402

Lincoln Park Conservation Assn.
741 Fullerton Ave.
Chicago, IL 60614

National Assn. of Housing
and Redevelopment Officials
2600 Virginia Ave., N.W.
Washington, DC 20037

National Trust for Historic Preservation
(headquarters)
740-748 Jackson Place, N.W.
Washington, DC 20006

> Mid-Atlantic Field Office
> (same as above)

> Midwest Regional Office
> 407 S. Dearborn St., Suite 710
> Chicago, IL 60605

> New England Field Service Office
> 141 Cambridge St.
> Boston, MS 02114

> Southern Field Office
> 456 King St.
> Charleston, SC 29403

> Southwest/Plains Field Office
> 903 Colcord Bldg.
> Oklahoma City, OK 73102

> Western Regional Office
> 681 Market St., Suite 859
> San Francisco, CA 94105

New Haven Redevelopment Agency
157 Church St.
New Haven, CT 06510

Old Neighborhood Assn.
Leo and Peg Pinard
714 Buchon St.
San Luis Obispo, CA 93401

Operation Clapboard—Oldport Assn.
Box 238
Newport, RI 02840

Pittsburgh History
and Landmarks Assn.
900 Benedum-Trees Bldg.
Pittsburgh, PA 15222

Providence Preservation Society
24 Meeting St.
Providence, RI 02903

Redevelopment Authority of
the City of Philadelphia
City Hall Annex
Philadelphia, PA 19107

San Francisco Redevelopment Agency
939 Ellis St.
San Francisco, CA 94109

The Society for Art
and Architectural Historians
1700 Walnut St., Room 716
Philadelphia, PA 19103

U.S. Dept. of Agriculture
Farmer's Home Administration
Washington, DC 20250

U.S. Dept. of Commerce
Economic Development Administration
Washington, DC 20230

U.S. Dept. of Housing
and Urban Development
Assistant Secretary for Community
Planning and Development
Washington, DC 20410

U.S. Dept. of Transportation
Assistant Secretary for Environment,
Safety and Consumer Affairs
Washington, DC 20590

U.S. General Services Administration
Historic Preservation Officer
Washington, DC 20405

West Philadelphia Corp.
4025 Chestnut St.
Philadelphia, PA 19104

Publications, Suppliers,
Manufacturers

Accurate Building Inspectors
4210 Ocean Ave.
Brooklyn, NY 11235

American Preservation Magazine
Bracy House
620 E. Sixth
Little Rock, AR 72202

Ceiling, Walls & More Inc.
124 Walnut St., P.O. Box 494
Jefferson, TX 75657

Focal Point Inc.
(mouldings)
Dept. O
2005 Marietta Rd., N.W.
Atlanta, GA 30318

JO-EL Light Shop
7120 Hawkins Creamery Rd.
Laytonsville, MD 20760

Levy's Gasolier Antiques
Box 627
Washington, DC 20044

Northeast American Heritage Co.
77 Washington St., N., Suite 502
Boston, MA 02114

The Old-House Journal
69A Seventh Ave.
Brooklyn, NY 11217

Pompei Stained Glass Studio
455 High St. (Rt. 60)
Medford, MA 12156

Preservation Resource Center
Lake Shore Rd.
Essex, NY 12936

The Renovator's Supply
71A Northfield Rd.
Millers Falls, MA 01349

Royal Windyne Ltd.
(ceiling fans)
1316 W. Main St., Dept JS
Richmond, VA 23220

San Francisco Victoriana
606 Natoma St.
San Francisco, CA 94103

Tremont Nail Co.
21 Elm St., P.O. Box 111
Wareham, MA 02571

The W.F. Norman Corp.
(metal ceilings)
P.O. Box 323-J
Nevada, MO 64772